MARKETING and SELLING YOUR FILM AROUND THE WORLD

MARKETING and SELLING YOUR FILM AROUND THE WORLD

AROUND THE WORLD

A GUIDE FOR INDEPENDENT FILMMAKERS

BY JOHN DURIE ANNIKA PHAM NEIL WATSON

SILMAN-JAMES PRESS   LOS ANGELES

First Edition

10 9 8 7 6 5 4 3 2 1

Library of Congress Cataloging-in-Publication Data
Durie, John.
Marketing and selling your film around the world : guide for independent filmmakers /
John Durie, Annika Pham, Neil Watson.–1st ed.
p. cm.
Includes bibliographical references.
1. Motion pictures–Marketing.   2. Motion pictures–Distribution.
I. Pham, Annika.   II. Watson, Neil.   III. Title.
PN1995.9.M29 D87 2000   384'.8'0688–dc21   00-023178

ISBN 1-879505-43-6

Cover design by Wade Lageose

Printed in the United States of America.

SILMAN-JAMES PRESS
1181 Angelo Drive
Beverly Hills, CA 90210

Contents

Acknowledgments ix

Foreword i

SECTION 1: FILM MARKETING: WHAT IS IT AND WHY IS IT NECESSARY? 1

Who Is the Target Audience? 3
Why Does a Film Need To Be Marketed? 3
What Is Film Marketing? 5

SECTION 2: THE CHANGING PATTERN OF CINEMAGOING IN EUROPE 7

The Need for New Investment–
  Protecting Production Investment 10
The Changing Shape of Spending on Movies 15
    Video 17
    TV and Pay-TV 17
    Cinemagoing 21

SECTION 3: INTERNATIONAL SALES 25

Financing and Distributing Films: An Overview 28
Independents 29
Development and Production Finance 29
What Is a Sales Agent? 29
Changes Within the International Sales Sector 31
Securing a Sales Agent 33
How Pre-Sales Work 33
Cross-Collateralization 35
How the Sales Agent Assesses The Marketplace 35
Assessing the Value of the Package 36
Ancillary Markets 38
Arranging the Finance 39
The Completion Guarantee 40

Strategies for Marketing to the Sales Agent 41
      Assembling the Package **42**
      Making the Approach **42**
      Crucial Ingredients **44**
          The Script **44**
          The Director **44**
          The Cast **44**

Preparing to Sell 46
      When a Synopsis Will Do **47**
      The Importance of the U.S. Deal **48**

SECTION 4: MARKETS AND FESTIVALS **51**

Working the Markets 56
Key Marketing Tools at the First Market 57
          The Shooting Script **57**
          The Synopsis **60**
          Stills, Filmographies, and
              Background Information **60**
      Publicity and Press **60**
      Announcing Ad **62**
      Trade Listings **62**
      Keeping in Touch **63**
Key Marketing Tools at the Second Market 64
      Delivery Date **64**
      The Office Display **64**
          The Poster **65**
          Stills **66**
          The Showreel **68**
          The Rough Cut of the Trailer **68**
          The Brochure **68**
Key Marketing Tools at the Third Market 69
      Trade Advertising **69**
      Market Screenings **70**
      Press Books **74**
      Marketing Budgets During Sales **75**
      Timing the Deal **75**
Festivals 76

SECTION 5: FILM DISTRIBUTION IN EUROPE 81

Key Concepts in Film Distribution 83
The Structure of Film Distribution in Europe 87
Economies of Scale 89
Concentration on a Few Star-Driven Titles 92
Positioning Pictures That Don't Fit Traditional
    Categories 95
Exploiting a Film's Assets 97
                Stars 97
                The Director 98
        Exploiting a Film's Genre and
            Story Ingredients 99
        Using Awards 100
        Exploiting Performances in
            Other Territories 102
Who Is the Target Audience for a Film? 103
Determining the Date and Pattern of a Film's Release 104
The Relationship Between Distributor and Exhibitor 104
Selecting a Release Date 108
        Time of Year 110
        Competition from Other Titles 110
        Using Key Dates in the Film Calendar 111
The Release 113
        Day-and-Date Release 113
        Platform Release 114
The Prints and Advertising Budget 117
                Print Costs 117
                Advertising Costs 118
                Publicity Costs 118
                Promotional Costs 118
        P&A Costs in Europe 120
        Dubbing and Subtitling Costs 121
The Essential Ingredients of an Advertising Campaign 123
        Overall Planning 123
                Photographs 124

viii

MARKETING AND
SELLING
YOUR FILM
AROUND THE
WORLD

Creating the Poster Art   **125**
> *Creating the Copy for the Poster*   **127**
> *Positioning the Poster*   **128**
> *Censorship*   **130**
Creating and Using the Trailer   **130**
> *Teaser Trailers*   **131**
> *Getting the Trailer Played*   **132**
Creating and Using Press Advertising   **133**
Creating and Using Websites   **134**
Creating and Using Television Advertising   **135**
Creating and Using Radio Advertising   **136**
Market Research   **136**
> *Playability*   **137**
> *Positioning*   **137**
> *Marketing Materials*   **138**
> *Release Date*   **138**
> *Media and Advertising*   **138**
The Publicity and the Promotional Campaign   **139**
Creating the Strategy   **141**
The Press Kit's Ingredients   **142**
The Importance of Star Interviews   **142**
Press Screenings   **143**
Preview Screenings   **144**
Gala Premieres   **146**
Merchandising Campaigns   **146**
Sponsorship   **148**

SECTION 6: EXHIBITION IN EUROPE   **149**

New Cinemas, Rising Admissions   **151**
The Introduction of the Multiplex   **151**
The Multiplexes' Impact on
    Film Distribution   **153**
The Nature of the Multiplex   **154**
Marketing Strategies   **156**
Reporting   **162**
Net Rentals   **163**

ACKNOWLEDGMENTS

The authors would like to thank the following film industry professionals who set aside time from often hectic schedules for interviews that provided invaluable source material for the first edition of this book.

This information has been updated and added to through the authors' experience, research, and further interviews to reflect the changes in the industry since the original publication, which was entitled *The Film Marketing Handbook*.

Thierry Abel
Daniel Battsek
Karl Baumgarten
Simona Benzakein
Tim Bevan
Patrizia Biancamano
Monique Bondil
Stephen Burdge
Martin Butterworth
Norma Cairns
Helene Cardis
Maurizio della Casa
Philippe de Chaisemartin
Denis Chateau
Adriana Chiesa
Bo Christensen
Roberto Cimpanelli
Duncan Clark
Dennis Davidson
John Dick
Erwin Dietrich

Eliane Dubois
Lena Enquist
Andi Engel
Stan Fishman
Peter Fornstam
Tullio Galleno
Dany Geys
Andrés Vicente Gómez
Bruno Gosse
Thomas Halbere
Joseph Helfgot
Alexandre Heylen
Paco Hoyos
Bernadette Icovic
Gilles Jacob
Ralph Kamp
Chris Koppelmeier
Jean Labadie
Pierre Ange LePogam
Elena Lloyd
Michel Luel

San Fu Maltha

Enrique Gonzalez Macho

Jean-Rene Marchand

Pandelis Mitropoulos

Wendy Palmer

Valerio de Paolis

Alberto Pasquale

Tracy Payne

Gerhard Pedersen

Pedro Perez

Peter Philipsen

Sandro Pierotti

Claude-Eric Poiroux

Peter Refn

Renate Rose

Arnaud Rouvilloix

Mike Ryan

Bertil Sandgren

Marc Samuelson

Bill Stephens

Ute Schneider

Hy Smith

Per Tengblad

Simon Ubsdell

Tharci Vanhuysse

Jan Verheyen

Jose Vicuna

Herman Weigel

Wim van Wouw

Anke Zindler

The authors would also like to acknowledge the generous assistance, encouragement, and support by a number of other people throughout the gestation of this book:

At the Media Business School, the former general managers Gudie Lawaetz and Fernando Labrada and, in particular, the current general manager Antonio Saura, who nurtured the project and provided enthusiastic backing. Without their support and that of the MEDIA program of the European Union, the original publication would not have reached fruition.

Ben Keen and the editorial team at *Screen Digest* kindly allowed us to reproduce statistical data from their publication.

At Silman-James, we wish to thank Jim Fox for his patience, guidance, and ideas and also Gwen Feldman.

We also thank Denise Brown and the staff at Carroll & Brown in London for their efforts in regard to the original European edition of this publication.

FOREWORD

Getting a film onto a cinema screen is a process that comprises many distinct but interlinked stages, including financing, production, and distribution, each of which requires its own specialized talent and expertise.

However, the one common link that unites all the different stages of a film's life is marketing. The target audience may change at each stage: When a film is being sold to the industry, the marketing is aimed at international distributors. When a film is finally distributed, the goal is to reach the cinemagoing public. But whether the task is the preparation of a synopsis designed to raise the interest of potential financiers, the arranging of a screening to industry and press at the Cannes Film Festival, or the making a trailer for the general public, marketing is involved at each step.

Thus, for every type of film, ranging from large mainstream releases to specialized arthouse pictures, a marketing strategy must be created and executed, using a set of established tools. The film business is dependent on persuading distributors to pay money to acquire rights to pictures and enticing the public to buy cinema tickets. The marketing strategy for a film plays a crucial role in determining the success of this process.

In *Marketing and Selling Your Film Around the World*, we start from the basic concepts of feature-film marketing and attempt to show how to create marketing strategies that will use these tools in the most effective way at each stage of a film's life.

Successful film marketing is often assumed to be dependent on the strength of a single creative idea. While not disputing the importance of such ideas as a trailer or a poster, this book tries to demonstrate how all marketing ideas will only be effective if they are incorporated into a focused but flexible marketing plan that is based on a realistic budget.

Film marketing is not an exact science, but proper planning, which allows sufficient time for the preparation of all necessary materials, will greatly increase a marketing effort's chances of attaining its desired goals and help minimize the risk of costly mistakes. This is of particular importance to independent producers who wish to sell their films to independent distributors around the world, either directly or through an international sales agent.

This book evolved from the work of the Media Business School (MBS), an initiative of the MEDIA Program created by the European Community to assist the development of the European audiovisual industry. One of the primary objectives of the MBS is to create a forum that benefits European filmmakers at every stage of their careers. This book forms part of that effort.

The MBS continues to be the pre-eminent training ground for European film professionals. Using the very best international professionals as acting lecturers and guest speakers, the MBS runs a series of short workshops and long-term training programs aimed at increasing the business expertise for today's film and television producers.

Marketing and Selling Your Film Around the World focuses primarily on the marketing and distribution of independent films in Europe, although the sections on international sales, markets, and festivals will be applicable to any independent film, regardless of country of origin or size of budget.

The first edition of this book was based on interviews with more than 80 senior figures involved in all aspects of film marketing in fourteen European countries. In this update, we have included new information and examples to benefit independent filmmakers seeking to get their films from the production stage through to international distributors and, ultimately, to the cinemagoing public.

Marketing and Selling Your Film Around the World is designed to allow readers to dip in and out of its various sections, each of which addresses marketing at a different stage of a film's life. In effect, it is rather like a cookbook. You, the reader, are the chef, selecting the particular ingredients that you believe will work most successfully for your film at a given time. Since every film is composed of a different set of elements, the overall effect is like trying a new recipe each time, and it will be impossible to predict the results until the film reaches its final customer–the paying public. I wish you good cooking.

John Durie

FILM MARKETING: WHAT IS IT AND WHY IS IT NECESSARY?

While awareness of the tools of film marketing is important, such knowledge is of limited use unless it is accompanied by a detailed understanding of how to use these tools in an effective way, as part of a coherent, cost-effective strategy.

In the international film industry, awareness and knowledge of the importance of film marketing continues to increase. This is partly because of the escalating costs of releasing films, which has meant that companies are eager to ensure that their money is spent in the most cost-effective way. The increasing sophistication of many marketing campaigns means that, unless a given film avails itself of an effective marketing strategy, its chances of earning its money back in a crowded marketplace are considerably diminished.

■ Who Is the Target Audience?

This book is concerned with the marketing and distribution of independent films, as opposed to those handled by the Hollywood majors. Independent pictures have, in effect, two target audiences for the marketing process.

The first target audience is the international distributor, also known as the buyer–without a distributor, a picture will not be released. Once a film has been sold to a distributor, the target audience becomes the cinemagoer, who must be persuaded to purchase a ticket to see the film.

■ Why Does a Film Need To Be Marketed?

One sector of the film industry argues that a film does not need to be marketed, since it is art, the intrinsic value of which will be instinctively recognized by its audience. This argument assumes that film is not a product like soap powder, which needs to be actively marketed to persuade the public to buy it. The very word "product" is felt to demean a film's artistic status. While such an argument is often a manifestation of the passion that people inside the industry feel for films, it runs the risk of ignoring certain key aspects of the way in which films are put together and of ignoring the workings of the marketplace. Filmmakers from this sector of the industry are often involved in making films that have an emphasis on a cultural slant, rather than commercial one, or working with heavily subsidized productions.

Regardless of a filmmaker's motive, a film—whether it's aimed at attracting the widest possible audience at home and abroad or aimed at a very specific minority—is only produced after a lengthy gestation period. During this time, considerable energy is expended in seeking to ensure that the film will be attractive to a target audience, however that audience is defined—and often in an extremely competitive marketplace.

In these terms, a film does have the status of a product, which, like many other products, passes through a phase of research and development, during which the aim is to orientate it toward a particular market.

Selling to international buyers or to the public ultimately depends on creating something that people are prepared to risk money to distribute or which people are prepared to pay to see at the cinema. Indeed, even the most esoteric film is made for a paying audience, be it at a cinema or at home on video or broadcast television. As such, a film is a leisure activity that uses people's disposable time and income. Marketing a film to the public involves competing not only with other films, but with other types of leisure activities that vie for the public's disposable income.

> *" The goal of marketing is to maximize a film's audience and, by extension, its earning potential. "*

The premise that forms the backbone of this book is that the goal of marketing is to maximize a film's audience and, by extension, its earning potential. There is no intention to prescribe the kinds of films that could or should be made. Rather, the intention is simply to underline the fact that film is a business in which companies are driven by the need to make a profit in order to continue their business of producing more films in the future. Marketing is an essential part of this process.

■ What Is Film Marketing?

Throughout this book, film marketing is defined as any activity that assists a film in reaching its target audience at any time throughout its life. To achieve this, a marketing strategy must be constructed, a strategy that creates marketing tools and uses them in the most effective manner possible. As such, the marketing strategy will incorporate elements as diverse as print designs (e.g., posters), trailers and show-

> *" A film can be defined as a one-off purchase. "*

reels, publicity, advertising, promotion, and merchandising.

In the film industry, what is often being sold is an idea, a concept that the buyer wants to believe is going to be exciting, enjoyable—desired by an audience, big or small. Every film, whatever its inherent merit, is a unique creation, since it will contain a mix of different elements that have never before been put together in quite that way, and which will never be repeated in quite that way again. Thus, each film may be defined as a prototype. When people buy a product that is new to them, they may first engage in the process of sample testing (for example, trying on several pairs of jeans). In the case of toothpaste or soft drinks, the consumer may buy several different brands before settling on a favorite. By contrast, an audience cannot closely compare a new film with another existing product and will not be able to sample it fully, except by paying to see it. Therefore, a film can be defined as a one-off purchase, not a repeat purchase as with many other products.

An audience searches for perceived hallmarks of quality and may, of course, decide to see a certain film based on its genre or the name of its director or star. However, because a film's actual quality depends on a mix of numerous variables, such a decision does not guarantee consumer satisfaction. To minimize the chances of wasting time and money on a bad film, an audience may also seek information prior to purchase through word of mouth, reviews, and advertising.

However, before being sold to the general public, a film has to be sold to an international distributor. Here, time is critical. As we shall see in Section 3 (International Sales), a company selling a film to international distributors has only a limited amount of time in which to convince them to purchase it. This period—a film's shelf-life—will climax with the screening of the finished film. Few films increase in value once they have been screened. The goal of the company representing a film is to sell it at the time when its value is at its maximum. When a film has recognizable elements, such as a known director and cast, its maximum value may be prior to its completion. If a film doesn't have such recognizable elements, the majority of the selling will take place once it is completed and screened to buyers (see Section 4, Markets and Festivals).

Once a film is released to the general public, it again has a limited shelf-life. Rarely will a film increase its box-office value once it has been released. Therefore, the focus of the marketing strategy will be the film's release date, with the aim of maintaining interest for as long as possible following its debut in the marketplace.

To plan an effective marketing strategy, understanding the overall environment in which the campaign will be executed is crucial. The following section examines the changing nature of the European marketplace and why these changes have made marketing so important.

THE CHANGING PATTERN OF CINEMAGOING IN EUROPE

Since the early 1950s, the nature of cinemagoing in Europe has undergone dramatic changes. Whereas a visit to the cinema was once regarded as a mass activity that the public would undertake with relatively little persuasion, an explosion in the variety of other available leisure pursuits has meant that getting people to pay to see films requires much greater effort. The rapid growth of new television channels has also meant that consumers now have access to a cheap and convenient alternative source of audiovisual entertainment.

Changes in lifestyle patterns have also had a dramatic impact on cinemagoing patterns. As a result of the post-war "baby boom," young parents increasingly preferred to stay at home with their children rather than trekking into town centers for their entertainment. This "baby boom" phenomenon occurred in both North America and Europe. In the United States, it started almost immediately after the war, but in most European countries, it did not really become apparent until the early 1960s. This was primarily because the United States emerged from the war economically buoyant, while much of Europe had been ravaged, and its economies took longer to recover. For this reason, the American film business adjusted to the changing nature of the audience faster than the industry in Europe.

Faced with the decline in the audience, both the American and the European film industries were forced to acknowledge that they had to work harder to attract people to the cinema. Therefore, in both North America and Europe, film marketing assumed a much greater importance and a marked increase in sophistication. But the problems and strategies faced on the two sides of the Atlantic were somewhat different.

> *"The American film business adjusted to the changing nature of the audience faster than the industry in Europe."*

In Europe, six key changes in cinemagoing patterns have had a direct impact on the nature and scope of film marketing:

1) A decline in the number of screens, followed by investment in new multiplex screens;

2) A decline in cinema admissions, then a rise as a result of investment in new multiplexes;

3) A rise in ancillary media;

4) A change in the public's leisure patterns;

5) A change in audience demographics;

6) A decline and subsequent rise in the market share of European films.

According to figures from the U.K.-based monthly trade publication *Screen Digest*, in 1960, 2.9 billion cinema tickets were sold in the countries that now make up the European Community. By 1990, the number of tickets sold in those same countries had fallen to just 564 million.

■ The Need for New Investment— Protecting Production Investment

In the mid-1980s, an ambitious program of investment in new multiplexes began in Europe. This investment was largely led by such American companies as AMC, Warner Bros., and United Cinemas International (a joint venture between Paramount and MCA). They recognized that European cinemas had been allowed to fall into a perilous state as a result of the failure of their owners to refurbish the interiors and invest in such basic items as new seating. In addition, standards of service were often appalling and information about the films playing was difficult to obtain.

As a result, between the mid-1980s and the mid-1990s, sources estimate that total investment in multiplexes in the U.K. alone was over $1.65 billion–the vast majority of this being American money.[1] The fact that this investment was largely financed by American companies was a reflection of their ability to anticipate audience demand, while their ability to make those venues a success through sophisticated retail techniques was a testament to their marketing skills.

By 1993, the downward trend in European cinema attendance had been reversed and admissions began to rise again. By 1997, the cinemagoing habit had returned and admissions across the European Union (E.U.) had risen to 758.5 million.[2] (See chart one, Cinema Admissions.)

Screen Digest reports that, in 1990, each European visited the cinema on average 1.9 times–just one-sixth of the figure for 1960–and spent an average of nine dollars. By contrast, in the U.S., the habit of cinemagoing remained relatively strong, with 4.2 visits per year per capita in 1990 and an average per-head spending of $21–more than double the Western European average. (See chart two, Cinemagoing per Capita.) In 1997, the average number of annual per-capita cinema visits in the E.U. was still less than half the U.S. average–2.3 against 5.16. Measured by total admissions, with 1.3 billion tickets sold in 1997, the U.S. market was twice as large as the market across the European Union (758.5 million).

The decline in admissions in Europe between 1960 and 1990 led to the closure of many cinema screens–over this period, a 60% decrease in screen capacity was registered across Europe. As a result, many people found it more difficult to locate a cinema in their own neighborhood, which served as a further disincentive for going to see films. However, the building of multiplexes in Europe, which began during the mid-1980s, produced a rise in the number of screens. (See Chart 3, Cinema Screens in the E.U., Canada, and the USA between 1960 and 1997.)

---

[1] For more information on multiplexes see Section 6.
[2] In the meantime, three new countries–Austria, Finland, and Sweden– had been admitted to the European Union, but this in itself made a relatively small contribution to the greater volume of admissions. Far more important was the increase in the overall admissions.

CHART 1

Cinema Admissions in the E.U., the U.S. and Canada (millions)

SOURCE: Screen Digest

COUNTRIES	1995	1996	1997
AUSTRIA	11.99	12.32	13.72
BELGIUM	19.24	21.21	22.07
DENMARK	8.82	9.89	10.84
FINLAND	5.3	5.49	5.9
FRANCE	13.24	136.62	148.13
GERMANY	124.49	132.89	143.12
GREECE	10.2	8.4	10.5
IRELAND	9.84	11.48	11.49
ITALY	90.7	95.9	100.37
LUXEMBOURG	0.67	0.75	0.85
NETHERLANDS	17.18	16.8	18.9
PORTUGAL	12	11.5	13.5
SPAIN	94	104.26	105.04
SWEDEN	15.56	15.21	15.21
U.K.	116.13	125.08	138.92
Total E.U.	666.35	707.81	758.57
Canada	87.45	90.12	98.14
USA	1.262.60	1.338.60	1.387.70

CHART 2

Average Cinemagoing Per Capita in the E.U. and the U.S.

SOURCE: Screen Digest

	1960	1980	1990	1995	1997
BELGIUM	8.8	2.2	1.6	1.9	2.1
DENMARK	9.7	3.1	1.9	1.7	2.07
FRANCE	7.8	3.3	2.2	2.2	2.51
GERMANY	11.4	2.3	1.7	1.5	1.73
GREECE	8	4.8	1.6	1	0.99
IRELAND	13.1	3.2	2.1	2.6	3.21
ITALY	14.7	4.3	1.6	1.6	1.76
LUXEMBOURG	14.2	2.3	1.3	1.7	2.03
NETHERLANDS	4.8	2	1	1.1	1.2
PORTUGAL	2.9	3.3	1	1.1	1.3
SPAIN	12.5	4.9	2	2.3	2.66
U.K.	9.6	1.8	1.7	1.9	2.35
EUR 12 (from 1986)	10.5	3.2	1.9		
AUSTRIA	15.3	2.3	1.3	1.6	1.6
FINLAND	5.6	2.1	1.2	1	1.14
SWEDEN	6.7	3	1.8	1.8	1.7
EUR 15 (from 1995)	1.6	1.7	1.9		
U.S.	7.5	4.7	4.2	4.7	5.16

CHART 3

Cinema Screens in the E.U., Canada and the USA (1960-1997)

SOURCE: Screen Digest

COUNTRIES	1960	1970	1980	1990	1996	1997
BELGIUM	1,550	800	508	461	440	447
DENMARK	500	390	475	347	322	328
FRANCE	5,834	4,274	4,540	4,518	4,529	4,655
GERMANY	6,950	3,673	3,418	3,754	4,035	4,128
GREECE	1,000	1,034	1,103	500	320	330
IRELAND	290	240	163	171	218	234
ITALY	10,517	9,439	8,453	3,249	3,640	3,665
LUXEMBOURG	35	25	20	17	16	16
NETHERLANDS	565	435	523	423	435	501
PORTUGAL	500	500	423	250	303	322
SPAIN	6,459	6,827	4,096	1,773	2,354	2,565
U.K.	3,034	1,529	1,530	1,685	2,215	2,383
EUR 12	37,110	29,166	25,300	17,148	18,406	19,150
AUSTRIA	1,275	770	511	393	421	424
FINLAND	610	330	352	340	325	322
SWEDEN	2,500	1,357	1,239	1,138	1,169	1,174
EUR 15	41,495	31,623	27,402	19,019	20,321	21,070
CANADA	1,278	1,156	1,037	1,713	2,034	2,164
USA	16,354	14,000	17,590	23,689	29,731	31,640

The growth of the video market and the deregulation of television have also had a major impact on film-consumption patterns in Europe, resulting in an overall expansion in the demand for filmed entertainment.

■ The Changing Shape of Spending on Movies

The global market for audiovisual products is expanding at an exponential rate. Such new technologies as pay-per-view and DVD–which depend heavily on feature films–are producing a huge increase in consumer expenditure on audiovisual product. Even allowing for inflation, U.K. consumer expenditure on films alone increased by 750% between 1981 and 1997.

The introduction of digital technology is rapidly erasing the distinctions between the television, the computer, and the telecom industries, since they increasingly utilize common production and distribution mechanisms. The film industry, as the creator and distributor of "high-value software," will play a vital role in this convergence of delivery systems. However, only those companies that have developed sufficient critical mass, buttressed by a strong capital base, will really be in a position to exploit this convergence.

> *"The growth of ancillary media has had an extraordinary impact on patterns of spending on feature films in both Europe and the U.S."*

The growth of ancillary media has had an extraordinary impact on patterns of spending on feature films in both Europe and the U.S. Overall expenditure has risen sharply as new forms of distribution have emerged, and the way in which money is spent has undergone a dramatic change. As recently as the mid-1970s, sales of cinema tickets accounted for 100% of direct consumer

CHART 4

Percentage of Expenditure on Feature Films in Some Key E.U. Countries and in the U.S. (1996)

SOURCE: Screen Digest

	Theatrical	Video rental	Video sell through	Pay-TV
FRANCE	26.8	6.5	18.7	48
GERMANY	41.4	16.3	23.5	18.7
U.K.	19.3	19.2	19.7	41.7
E.U.	31.3	14.2	20.4	34
U.S.	23.9	32.4	19.7	21.9

CHART 5

Average Weekly Expenditure on Leisure Services in the U.K. (96/97)

SOURCE: U.K. Office for National Statistics

LEISURE SERVICES	£
Cinema admissions	0.28
Theatre, concerts, circus, amateur shows	0.59
Sports admissions and subscriptions	2.19
TV, video, satellite rental, TV license	3.26
Miscellaneous entertainments	1.04
Educational and training expenses	4.55
Holiday in U.K.	2.41
Holiday abroad	7.45
Other incidental holiday expenses	3.37
Gambling payments	3.82
Cash gifts, donations	5.00

expenditure on movies. But by 1996, subscriptions from pay-TV accounted for 34% of total movie spending and receipts from the theatrical box office for about 31.3%, while video sell-through accounted for 20.4% and video rental for 14.2% (See Chart 4, Percent of Expenditure on Feature Films in Some Key E.U. Countries and in the U.S., and Chart 5, Average Weekly Expenditure on Leisure Services in the U.K.)

Video

Video first emerged as an important medium for viewing feature films during the early 1980s. Initially, the rental of videos was the principal source of revenue from this sector. Rental is still the primary source of revenue from video in many European countries, but the purchase of tapes by the consumer, known as video sell-through, has become increasingly prevalent, although special-interest tapes (featuring sports, leisure activities, and children's programs, rather than feature films) have become this sector's driving force. The sell-through sector is particularly strong in the U.K., France, Germany, and Italy. By 1996, the overall value of the sell-through market in the European Union had risen to approximately $2.8 billion, although its growth had slowed considerably, while the rental market remained steady at around $1.9 billion. The development of pay-TV in the 1990s was one of the main factors that helped to slow video's sell-through growth. (See Chart 6.)

As in the rest of the world, most E.U. countries adopted a six- to twelve-month window between theatrical and video release dates to ensure that theatrical revenues did not suffer as a result of the growth of video. (See Chart 7, Release Windows.) However, even with such a window in operation, consumers know that if they wait a few months after a film's theatrical release, they can view that film on video for much less than the cost of a cinema ticket–cost being widely cited by the public as a deterrent against visiting the cinema.

CHART 6

Spending on the Movies in Millions of U.S. Dollars Exchanged at Constant 1996 Rate

SOURCE: Screen Digest

	1988	1990	1994	1995	1996
FRANCE					
theatrical	701	739	828	871	933
video rental	174	209	184	191	226
video sell-through	78	247	501	567	652
pay-TV	825	1095	484	1582	1673
GERMANY					
theatrical	537	541	803	773	931
video rental	549	462	329	339	366
video sell-through	50	137	441	490	529
pay-TV	7	12	266	327	421
ITALY					
theatrical	339	399	541	521	566
video rental	95	95	94	88	95
video sell-through	22	101	300	244	246
pay-TV	0	0	173	209	236
SPAIN					
theatrical	179	220	338	375	454
video rental	308	248	94	98	108
video sell-through	9	37	161	197	208
pay-TV	0	3	285	358	445

CHART 6 (continued)

U.K.

theatrical	302	423	632	623	704
video rental	672	793	616	643	701
video sell-through	144	281	595	684	719
pay-TV	0	146	917	1193	1519

Total E.U.

theatrical	2,565	2,857	3,830	3,859	4,346
video rental	2,495	2,406	1,779	1,819	1,967
video sell-through	320	904	2,380	2,604	2,835
pay-TV	871	1,367	3,532	4,094	4,717

USA

theatrical	4,458	5,022	5,396	5,494	5,944
video rental	6,061	7,551	8,564	8,160	8,078
video sell-through	1,469	2,346	3,683	4,384	5,436
pay-TV	4,215	4,842	4,586	5,157	5,448

TV and Pay-TV

Alongside video, the deregulation of television, brought about as European governments allowed private operators to challenge state monopolies, created an additional medium for the viewing of feature films. Pay-TV–which requires consumers to pay a monthly subscription fee to receive a particular television channel–became a main factor in the increased consumer demand for feature films. Between 1988 and 1996, the number of European pay-TV subscribers increased dramatically. In particular, the French pay-TV service Canal+, which also has stakes in pay services in Italy, Belgium, Germany, and Spain, and BSkyB in the U.K. have been driving forces in the growth of such channels, which have contributed to the increase in overall spending on filmed entertainment in Europe.

CHART 7

Release Windows in E.C. Countries

SOURCE: Espace Video Européen / authors' research

	VIDEO	TELEVISION
BELGIUM	Informal agreements used for Flemish-speaking region French regulations used for French-speaking region	
DENMARK	6 months 1 year for local films	18 months
FRANCE	1 year	1 year for pay-TV 2 years for free-TV
GERMANY	6 months	18 months for pay-TV 2 years for free-TV
GREECE	6-12 months	30 months
IRELAND	6-12 months	12-18 months for pay-TV 2-3 years for free-TV
ITALY	9 months	15 months for pay-TV 2 years for free-TV
LUXEMBOURG	— Informal agreements used —	
NETHERLANDS	6 months	18 months for pay-TV 2 years for free-TV
PORTUGAL	1 year	2 years
SPAIN	6-8 months	6-12 months
U.K.	6 months for rental 1 year for sell-through	1 year for pay-TV 2 years for free-TV

The development of new digital technologies is likely to have a dramatic impact on the television landscape. Digital compression of transmission signals allows a single satellite to broadcast hundreds of channels, many of which are likely to be dedicated to movies. Digital services were introduced in Germany and France in 1997, and other countries are set to follow suit.

The types of films that succeed in these ancillary markets are invariably the same types that succeed in the theater—the so-called "A titles," whose principal ingredients are recognized stars and quality production values. Since the marketing campaign for a film's theatrical release has a relatively high profile, it also acts as an essential tool in creating consumer interest in a film in these ancillary markets. In fact, those who buy films for these ancillary media often insist that the theatrical distributors of the films they purchase commit to a minimum spend on prints and advertising (P&A) for theatrical release. This is done to boost the profile of a film so that it may attract more interest on video and television.

> *" Even with the development of new digital technologies, theatrical marketing will probably remain the key to other markets because of its high profile. "*

Even with the development of new digital technologies that will permit so-called "video-on-demand" or "near video-on-demand," which will enable films to be delivered to the home via the telephone lines, theatrical marketing will probably remain the key to other markets because of its high profile.

Cinemagoing

Despite the strength of the ancillary markets, a visit to the cinema is likely to retain its appeal for many people because the experience of going to see a film on the big screen with an audience is

CHART 8

Market Share of National and U.S. Films in Five Key E.U. Countries (in percentages)

SOURCE: CNC/Screen Digest/trade magazines

	1990	1994	1995	1996	1997
FRANCE					
national	37.5	28.3	35.2	37.5	34
U.S.	55.9	60.9	53.9	54.3	55
GERMANY					
national	9.7	10.1	6.3	16.2	17.3
U.S.	83.8	81.6	87.1	75.1	70
ITALY					
national	21	23.7	21.1	27	31.3
U.S.	70	61.4	63.2	74	48.7
SPAIN					
national	10.4	7.1	11.9	9.3	15
U.S.	72.5	72.3	72.1	78.2	67
U.K.					
national	7	10.5	8.6	11.8	19.9
U.S.	89	85.6	83.7	81.7	73.5

an event that cannot be replicated by viewing a film on television, no matter how sophisticated that television viewing becomes.

In addition to its competition with a variety of different media, cinemagoing competes for the public's time and money with a growing number of other leisure pursuits. As working hours have decreased in Europe over the past few years, a new leisure economy that places an increasing importance on such activities as eating out, attending sports events, and going to nightclubs has emerged.

Between 1981 and 1991, the decline in European cinema attendance was mirrored by a sharp decline in the popularity of European films. Meanwhile, films originating in the U.S. consistently maintained their level of popularity, so that the net effect has been an increase in their percentage share of the box office at the expense of European films. By 1990, films of U.S. origin had increased their European box-office share to as much as 80% in many countries, while this figure reached 89% in the U.K. (See Chart 8, Market Share of National and U.S. Films in Five Key E.U. Countries.)

A wide variety of reasons have been offered for the diminishing popularity of local films. Some observers point to a decline in productions rooted in a specific culture while others argue that European productions have failed to adapt to changing audience tastes. But by 1995, there were signs that this trend was being partly reversed in some countries because a new breed of entrepreneurial producers, with one eye firmly on consumer tastes, were beginning to create films that captured the imagination of both local and international audiences. Examples of such films would include the English-language films *Four Weddings and a Funeral, Trainspotting,* and *The Full Monty* and non-English-language films *Il Postino* and *Life is Beautiful.*

Many European producers have also adopted a more sophisticated approach to marketing. This is particularly true for those films that have financial support from American distributors who fine-tune their films through recruited-audience screenings, which many traditional European professionals of the "auteur" school resist. The impact of the growth of multiplexes has undoubtedly also played its part in encouraging a newly entrepreneurial approach to the commercial potentials of film.

INTERNATIONAL SALES

Section 3

The task of marketing often begins when a producer first sells a film idea to potential financiers who will put up the money to fund the project.

Like all aspects of film marketing and distribution, the ultimate goal of international sales is maximizing profit. To achieve that end, sales companies use well-established, sometimes complex financing mechanisms. Therefore, if producers choose to finance or part-finance a picture through the sales route, they should use an established sales agent rather than attempt the task themselves or simply hand the job to enthusiastic friends in the industry.

Selling pictures is a specialized business that requires a comprehensive knowledge of distributors and market trends. Novice producers who ignore established procedures and conduct their own international sales could fast find themselves both out of their depth and out of pocket.

This section outlines the most effective procedures for attracting a sales agent's interest and explains how a sales agent markets a film in such a way as to maximize the interest of international distributors, who are also known as buyers. But before doing so, it is necessary to explain the environment in which the international sales agent operates.

> *" Selling pictures is a specialized business that requires a comprehensive knowledge of distributors and market trends. "*

Financing and Distributing Films: An Overview

From a business perspective, the key difference between most European and U.S. films is the manner in which they are financed. In the U.S., the majority of mainstream theatrical films are developed, financed, and distributed by one of the major Hollywood studios.[1] In some cases, such films will also be shown in a cinema chain in which the respective Hollywood major has an interest.

The majors, which are all owned by large conglomerates, have sufficient capital resources to handle all stages of the filmmaking process under one roof. This ability to handle the entire process of film-making—from the development of the original idea through to the distribution of the finished picture—gives these studios enormous marketing advantages. From the earliest possible moment, and certainly by the time an initial version of the script is ready, these studios' large and highly informed marketing and distribution departments are involved in putting together marketing-campaign ideas.

In some instances, these companies' overseas distribution arms may be asked to contribute ideas on casting and even to comment on a script to ensure that its idiosyncrasies will be acceptable to foreign audiences. These studios will also attempt to calculate a film's box-office potential based on the track records of its stars, director, and genre in certain territories.

---

[1] The term "Hollywood majors" usually refers to the following companies: Columbia Pictures, Walt Disney, MGM, Paramount, 20th Century Fox, Universal, Fox, and Warner Bros.

■ Independents

Few companies anywhere in the world have the financial resources to compete with the Hollywood majors. The entry costs for a company that sought to create an operation to rival the majors would be astronomical.

■ Development and Production Finance

Development money to assist in script development is usually the most difficult to secure, and, unless a project has a strong script with one or two key selling elements attached, it is unlikely to attract much attention from the industry's key players.

To raise production financing, producers and production companies will usually seek to sell their films to foreign distributors through either their own sales arms or companies that specialize in the international sales of feature films. These distributors, in turn, will sell a film's foreign rights in various media (theatrical, video, and various forms of television broadcast).

Pictures at the lowest end of the budget scale will be expected to recoup their costs primarily from their home territory. In such instances, foreign sales will simply be an additional revenue stream rather than a determinant of whether the film gets made at all.

■ What Is a Sales Agent?

Since few opportunities exist for independent films to be financed and distributed by a single entity, a number of mechanisms have been developed to expedite the process of raising funds for an independent production. The most common such mechanism is the use of an international sales company or sales agent to sell or license films to distributors in each international territory. (International sales agents are also sometimes referred to as international distributors. However, in strictest terms, an international distribution company is a group that is engaged in the distribution of films to cinema chains in several different countries).

These sales companies may have between five and thirty-five staff members, each of whom has a specialized knowledge (built up over many years) in evaluating the potential of scripts, directors, and casts and selling international rights for an intended or completed feature film to distributors around the world. These salespersons have long-term, established relationships with various distributors or buyers, which, in a competitive marketplace where relationships are paramount, can make a difference in securing a sale. Since sales agents sell four to twelve films per year, they carry considerable power with distributors, because they may be offering or already have sold a blockbuster film—something that all but a handful of top producers simply cannot duplicate.

Most sales agents also have close working relationships with such third-party financiers as banks, venture capital companies, state-supported funding agencies, and broadcasters. For this expertise, as well as for undertaking certain legal and technical responsibilities for the producer for an agreed period, a sales company will charge a commission that ranges between fifteen percent and twenty-five percent of revenues received, although some will go as low as ten percent.

> *"A producer must ensure that a sales agent is willing to take on some of the risk involved in trying to finance a picture."*

A producer must ensure that a sales agent is willing to take on some of the risk involved in trying to finance a picture. A sales agent should be prepared to bear some of the costs of marketing a film to international distributors, rather than allowing this burden to fall entirely on a film's producer. In this way, a sales agent will have some financial risk in a film and, therefore, an extra sales incentive.

Although sales agents may require a higher commission fee for such a contribution, their need to recoup their investments may impel them to be more motivated to sell a film.

■ Changes Within the International Sales Sector

International film sales is intensely competitive. Sales companies need movies to sell, and they rely predominately on their sales commissions from these movies to cover overhead and make a profit. Unless they have sufficient commercially attractive films, they will quickly go out of business.

Although the U.S. majors release their large blockbuster films through their own international distribution arms, they are also active in distributing more specialized films, backing a number of key sales and distribution companies such as Good Machine, backed by Universal, and Miramax, backed by Disney.

As a result, independent sales companies have become increasingly polarized in recent years. The bigger companies are becoming bigger, increasing the overall value of their film libraries, for which they continue to sell such ancillary rights as television and new technologies, by taking over smaller companies and selling eight to twelve new titles per year. Therefore, fewer sales agents are operating today, especially those who have the power to put up sufficient financing to assist a producer in getting a film into production.

Smaller, boutique agents remain very small, working with maybe two to five titles per year. To keep a steady supply of films, many sales companies are linked, either formally of through strong personal relationships, to independent producers and production companies.

Sales companies earn income on commission–the more they sell, the more they earn. However, this commission is earned not only on the new films that they present each year, but, as previously mentioned, also on older titles that can be re-issued for video, television, and other ancillary media.

A sales company's criteria for taking on a film will include considerations of a film's commercial potential, the time required to reach sales projections, the agents' relationships with a film's principals (director or producers), and whether the sales company likes the film.

All international sales companies have the same objective: to sell, and, if possible, pre-sell pictures to the international market. The sooner they can sell off the rights for the license fee they feel the film is worth (or what the buyers are willing to pay), the sooner they can recoup their investment, recover any marketing costs, and remit any balances to financiers and, eventually, producers.

After a film is released, the sales agent will collect monies from distributors, on behalf of the producer, and act as the producer's "caretaker" for the duration of the licensing period—usually fifteen years. Sales agents have considerably more negotiating power than producers because they are often able to tell the distributor that they will hold back delivery of any future pictures until they are paid all outstanding money. By contrast, producers will not usually have completed pictures that they can use as bargaining chips.

> "Sales agents have considerably more negotiating power than producers because they are often able to tell the distributor that they will hold back delivery of any future pictures until they are paid all outstanding money."

A number of leading international sales companies are based in London, which is a primary source for the financing of English-language pictures. They include such companies as Capitol Films, Film Four International, Icon, Intermedia, PolyGram, The Sales Company, and United Artists. A number of American-based independent sales companies also regularly seek films to sell to the world's distributors. Among the leaders are Miramax and Good Machine based out of New York, Lakeshore and Summit in Los Angeles, and

Alliance in Toronto. All of the above companies tend to deal with English-language pictures, although most of them have also handled prestige films made in other languages.

Among the European-based sales companies are the sales arms for French cinema giants Gaumont and Studio Canal+, the more specialized Dutch-based Fortissimo, Scandinavia's Nordisk Films, and Spain's Lola films.

■ Securing a Sales Agent

Securing a sales agent–particularly a good one–is one of the producer's primary tasks.

The international sales community is relatively small. According to Mike Ryan, co-chairman of J&M Entertainment, less than twenty international sales agents worldwide have enough clout to substantially enhance the power of a project. Competition for these agents' services is therefore fierce. Strategies for approaching them will be discussed in the next section.

■ How Pre–Sales Work

Film sales are of two types: the pre-sale, which is made before a film is completed and screened, and the straight sale, which is made once a film is completed and has been screened.

The key elements in the pre-sales system are the sales agent, the bank, and the distributors in key territories throughout the world. For the majority of films these key territories may be defined as the U.S., Canada, Australia, France, Germany, Italy, Japan, Scandinavia, Spain, and the U.K.

It is not the purpose of this book to explain all the possible scenarios that can occur when a film is pre-sold. The financing of films, particularly independent pictures, can be extremely complex. Since there is no such thing as standard product in the film industry, every picture tends to be financed in a different way.

> *"The financing of films, particularly independent pictures, can be extremely complex."*

In the simplest pre-sales scenario, a sales agent acting on behalf of a producer undertakes to sell a film to as many distributors worldwide as possible, either prior to the film commencing principal photography or while the film is shooting. (Many top-flight sales agents are only prepared to actively pitch a film if they are convinced that it will be produced and its cast and director are already in place.) And each distributor advances a specified sum of money to the sales agent once the distributor takes delivery of the completed film together with such materials as poster-ready artwork and a trailer. These funds that the distributor commits to advance on delivery are known as the *minimum guarantee.*

> *"Many top-flight sales agents are only prepared to actively pitch a film if they are convinced that it will be produced."*

Once a film is released in a particular territory, its returns to the distributor may exceed the original minimum guarantee paid. In this instance, the distributor will pay additional revenues, known as overages, to the sales agent at an agreed rate. These overages will be divided between the sales agent and the producer according to a specified formula.

A producer may have already attracted some equity investors in his or her film. Such investors will put up money in return for a share of the completed film's profits, if any. (Film is a high-risk industry and many pictures will fail to show a profit.) In such cases, pre-sales will be used to fund the shortfall between the equity finance already committed and the total budget. In other instances, it may be necessary to cover the whole budget from pre-sales.

■ Cross-Collateralization

The redistribution of earnings from theatrical distribution by the respective distributor in each territory can be made more complex by a common practice known as cross-collateralization, which can take many guises.

The *cross-collateralization of rights* allows a distributor to offset any losses incurred from a film's theatrical distribution against its profits from sales in such other media as video or television before distributing a share of the profits to the sales agent (and then the producer).

The *cross-collateralization of territories* is routinely used by the Hollywood majors. If a U.S. studio acquires international distribution rights to a picture, it will typically seek to cross-collateralize profits and losses among various territories. Under this arrangement, the film's producer will only be entitled to a share of the film's profits from a specific territory once the film's combined profits from all involved territories outweigh its combined losses.

The practice of cross-collateralizing packages of pictures so that profits from one producer's picture are set against losses from those of another producer is regarded with suspicion in most quarters.

■ How the Sales Agent Assesses the Marketplace

The minimum guarantee for an individual film in a specific territory will be subject to negotiation between the sales agent and the distributor. Prior to initially approaching distributors, the sales agent will usually have calculated a minimum and a maximum value to be expected from each major territory. These values are based on elements that include the budget of the film, the names of the director and the cast, and their track record at the box office in the territory concerned.

Although the term "sales" has wide currency in the industry, to say that a film is "licensed" is more accurate, since rights for a country are assigned to a distributor for a certain period of years—usually five to ten or fifteen years, depending on the territory and the strength of the distributor. After that time, a film's rights revert to the owner of the negative. In the case of most independent films, the owner will be the producer or the sales agent who has an agreement to license the film on behalf of the producer for a set number of years, usually twenty-five.

In some instances, the sales company itself will become a principal in the deal, agreeing to bankroll a production from its own credit lines in return for certain rights. This means that the producer will not have to wait for a lengthy and complex series of pre-sale agreements to be negotiated worldwide. In such cases, the sales agent will take a higher commission and may require an on-screen credit for sourcing production money for the producer. A sales company may also be involved in the packaging of a feature, for example, by helping to find a director and casting it.

Assessing the Value of the Package

To assess the likely value of a film in the marketplace, sales agents utilize a variety of research tools. Accessing this kind of information is frequently a time-consuming process because no single source of information exists for territories worldwide.

As part of this process, the sales agent will examine the specific marketplace performance of films within the same genre, the theatrical grosses achieved by previous films from a given director, and the video performance of this director's previous films in the specific territory. Another factor that the agent will consider is the current popularity of the cast and such key production people as the director of photography and the composer.

The sales agent must also determine how much financial return is likely to come from video and television sales and how much will come from the theatrical release.

Most sales companies build their files for projecting a film's performance by documenting the performances of various films in various media in the major territories, which is a specialized task that independent producers would have insufficient time and insufficient resources to do effectively. Sales agents assemble their projected figures by keeping abreast of the global box-office scene. This is done primarily by reading the trade papers. (The three main international trade papers are *Variety, Screen International,* and *The Hollywood Reporter.*) These trade papers can be used for tracking box-office performance, identifying generic trends in particular markets, and maintaining a daily awareness of what is performing well in the marketplace. In an effort to obtain the most comprehensive information possible, sales agents will supplement the information available in these three trade papers with information from other trades from various countries, such dedicated box-office information as that compiled by Entertainment Data Inc., and conversations with local distributors.

Many leading sales agents maintain a list of the top 100 stars and directors, and their relative popularity in various world markets, which enables these agents to make judgments about the value of specific individuals in specific markets. Sales agents will look at the elements in a picture and rate them on a sliding scale of value. In the case of most of the major territories, the attraction and value of a film is dependent on both the director and the cast.

A sales company's work is not over once a film is sold. The established sales companies must look after an inventory of pictures, which builds up over time. A company may have as many as 300 to 400 films in its library, with pictures turning over all the time. Even though a film may not have been shown theatrically for several years, sales companies will have to file royalty reports on it, calculating payments due to talent, based on television screenings in different countries around the world.

Sales agents will also constantly analyze the performance of various distributors in each territory, assessing the relative merits of each company in the handling of different types of films. Because the film industry is heavily dependent on personal contact, the departure of a key executive from a particular distributor may lead to a dramatic change in that company's fortunes, since, with the executive, may go a set of relationships that cannot easily be replaced. As a consequence, close monitoring of personnel changes is also critical.

Different sales agents specialize in different geographic areas. Their detailed knowledge of specific territories is usually gathered by talking to local distributors and other industry executives. An international sales agent's work entails year-round liaisons with the international community of distributors, maintaining contact via telephone, fax, e-mail, and overseas visits. The international sales community is a small one in which the maintenance of personal contact between sales agents and distributors is a fundamental aspect of the business. For mainstream pictures, the value of the principal territories, in terms of pre-sale contributions to the overall budget, generally adheres to the following approximate percentages: Australasia, two to three percent; France, six percent; Germany and Austria, ten percent; Italy, eight percent; Japan, ten to twelve percent; Spain, four percent; and the U.K., ten percent; although a particular film's casting and its director's track record might influence these figures to some degree.

> *" Personal contact between sales agents and distributors is a fundamental aspect of the business. "*

■ Ancillary Markets

In addition to assessing the financial value of a film's theatrical release, assessing a film's likely value in the ancillary markets of video and television is of great importance.

Determining the potential video revenue for a film in a specific territory is not a straightforward task. It depends on the video market of the country concerned and on the type of film being sold (small-, medium-, or big-budget). Information on a film's video performance is not easy to obtain.

With television sales, some seventy-five to eighty percent of the sales price will go to the sales agent, with the distributor retaining the remainder as a commission for selling the rights to local broadcasters. The sums remitted to the sales agent from these ancillary markets will be deducted from the minimum guarantee that the distributor has agreed to pay.

The practice of sub-distribution, under which a sales agent will appoint a local company in a specific territory to handle such ancillary sales as video and television, can be detrimental to a producer's interests. Such sub-distributors will themselves take a distribution fee, so that, in essence, the producer is obliged to pay twice over to secure a sale.

■ Arranging the Finance

Once a distributor has agreed to buy a picture from a sales agent, a contract will be drawn up between the sales company and the distributor. This contract will commit the distributor to advance the majority of the minimum guarantee upon delivery of the film, although a percentage may be paid when the contract is signed and when the film goes into production. (The term "delivery" has numerous definitions, but usually means the supply of a completed film—a print with married sound and picture and front and end credits.) Standard terms are usually twenty percent upon signature of the contract and eighty percent upon delivery of the completed film. However, if the film has been pre-bought or is unusually expensive, sales agents and distributors will normally agree to a series of staggered payments that are payable at different stages of production (e.g., a percentage at the start of principal photography, another amount at the end of shooting, and a final amount upon delivery).

This contract will usually include a letter of credit from the distributor's bank, in which the bank commits to advance the distributor the amount of the minimum guarantee at the required payment intervals.

Once all of a film's contracts, which usually amount to about fifteen to twenty different agreements, are in place, they are taken to one of a handful of banks that specialize in feature film financing, and, provided all the deals are with reputable companies, the bank will lend the producer the money required to cover the film's production costs. This practice is known as discounting pre-sale contracts. The creditworthiness of the distributor is clearly a key element in this process. Therefore, the banks that involve themselves with such agreements keep a close eye on the financial health of the various distributors around the world in an attempt to ensure that the distributors are able to meet their commitments to pay for the film on delivery.

In this financial scenario, the bank will charge interest on the money it advances to the producer (typically two to three percent above prime rates) as well as arrangement and management fees that may sometimes outweigh the interest charges because film production is a high-risk business.

■ The Completion Guarantee

A crucial element of this financial package is the completion guarantee, which is a form of insurance for the film's financiers. This guarantee is designed to protect the financiers in the event that the film runs over budget. The guarantor provides a bond, essentially cash, guaranteeing that the film will be delivered on time, on budget, and to the distributor's requirements. Should the film exceed its production costs, the guarantor is liable for the additional costs.

The guarantor charges the producer a fee in return for providing this security. Although no fixed rate for this service exists (the structure of every bond agreement is different and lower percentages are charged on high-budget films), up-front fees have tended to be in the 1.5% to 2% range in recent years, against an average of six percent ten years ago. Moreover, many producers have been seeking to exclude fixed costs, such as those for the script and director, from the budgetary total.

■ Strategies for Marketing to the Sales Agent

Competition to secure a sales agent is fierce. As they approach sales companies, producers must make their films stand out from the those produced by the large number of competing producers, all of whom are vying for the relatively few sales agents who can put up money to back a film's marketing campaign. Just as the process of marketing a film to audiences has firmly established ground rules, so the task of pitching a project to a sales agent has certain guidelines, which, if followed, give a producer a much greater chance of success.

Marketing a film to a sales agent is just as critical as marketing a film to the public. In many cases, pulling together the financing needed to start a production will be very difficult without a sales agent. This is especially the case where a limited production subsidy and private or institutional funding will be dependent on a loan against sales estimates, which normally have to be provided by a bona fide and accepted sales company.

Producers who start a project without the necessary funds or cash-flow are in an unfavorable position when seeking the last elements of financing, and in such cases often lose valuable sales or distribution rights.

Assembling the Package

The independent producer's first task is to excite the sales company about the picture for which finance is being sought. If the sales company is sufficiently excited by the film's script and its attached elements (such as its director and its potential cast), it may agree to represent the picture for foreign sales, thereby greatly enhancing the project's chances of finding the necessary financing.

> *" Although the best-known film-industry platitude is that 'nobody knows anything,' inside the industry there tends to be a consensus about exactly what kinds of projects can be pre-sold. "*

Although the best-known film-industry platitude is "nobody knows anything," particularly when it comes to predicting which films will succeed at the box office, inside the industry there tends to be a consensus about exactly what kinds of projects can be pre-sold. This is no guarantee that films that meet the guidelines of this consensus will go on to reap vast sums at the box office, but it does make it imperative that producers approaching industry sales agents do their homework and arrive with projects that have clearly defined pre-sale potential.

Making the Approach

The cold-selling of any product is always difficult; for a feature film it is virtually impossible. Sales agents invariably have established relationships with key producers who guarantee the agents a certain number of films to sell per year. For the sales agent, the risk inherent in taking on projects from people whom they do not know is simply too great to justify the time and expense involved. Therefore, agents will be very cautious about working with people with whom they have no prior relationship, unless those people come with strong personal recommendations from individuals whose judgments the agents implicitly trust.

In addition to the expenditures involved, a sales company will be putting its reputation on the line with each project that

> *" The cold-selling of any product is always difficult; for a feature film it is virtually impossible. "*

it backs. Since the world of international sales is a small, close-knit community, taking on just a handful of projects that it is unable to sell to foreign distributors could have a serious impact on a sales company's reputation. While it is by no means impossible for nascent producers to gain an entry to sales companies on their own, as with all communities of this sort, a personal introduction will invariably help open doors.

Ideally, the producer who approaches a sales company for the first time should have the backing of a respected film/TV agent, who will take a commission should the producer's project subsequently go into production. At the very least, the submission of the script should be

preceded by an introductory telephone call made by an industry figure who is known to both the sales agent and the producer. Such an individual ap-

> *" Every feature film has a shelf life and a sell-by date. "*

proach can help seduce the sales agent. "I like to think I'm being approached individually," says Mike Ryan of J&M Entertainment. "If I think everyone else is reading a script, I'm put off."

Reputable sales agents who sell feature films have a finite amount of time for the task. Every feature film has a shelf life and a sell-by date. As a business, sales agents usually select each of their six to twelve projects a year based on the project's potential sales revenue, the projects status and quality (e.g., Does it enhance the company itself?), and the project's key elements–director, cast, producer, script. However, some sales agents will sometimes consider unsolicited scripts if they are not gripped by the paranoia that has invaded the Hollywood studios, which simply return unsolicited scripts to the sender without opening them for fear that, if they even glance at them, they may later be sued for stealing an idea.

Crucial Ingredients

To excite a sales agent's interest in a project, a producer must provide a package containing certain basic ingredients. For most of the established sales agents the package must include the following:

The Script

This should embody an original and commercially accessible story. When submitted, the script should be accompanied by a one- to two-page synopsis (or, if possible, a treatment of the film) and an outlined financing plan that breaks down the film's budget and provides a provisional outline of how the proposed costs of the project will be covered. Where possible, a summary of the main characters, with the names of the actors and actresses being considered for the roles, should also be provided.

The Director

Ideally, a director with an established track record.

The Cast

Ideally, this list would include one or two well-known stars. A brief filmography of the principal confirmed members of the cast and crew can also be very helpful. If the producer has a track record, details of this will also be advantageous.

In many instances, the attachment of an established executive producer will substantially boost the chances of a film being taken on by a sales agent. The credibility of a project can also be boosted if its producer and its director have worked together on films that have achieved some level of success with the public. For example, producers Ted Hope and James Schamus from Good Machine have a close relationship with Ang Lee, as do Laurence Bender with Quentin Tarantino and Christine Vachon with Todd Haynes.

The more of these positive elements that are combined in a single package, the stronger the chances that that package (that film) will interest and possibly be acquired by a sales agent. While interest is the first step toward involving a sales agent in the financing

> " A project won't survive on interest alone. "

of a film, a project won't survive on interest alone. Converting this interest into a financial commitment is the producer's main task at this stage of the filmmaking process.

Some companies specialize in projects with "name" directors. United Artists, a specialist division of U.S. major MGM, tends to handle pictures from specific directors operating within defined styles, such as Pedro Almodovar, Mike Leigh, and David Lynch. Films that are heavily dependent on first-time talent will only be taken on in exceptional circumstances, although they can be made more attractive to a company if an experienced producer is attached.

In the arthouse sector, few films are pre-sold except on the basis of the director's name. Cast names are considered important, but only in relation to the key territories where a particular cast member may be well known.

In some instances, a film has a better chance of being picked up by a sales agent if the generic elements of the picture (e.g., whether it is a comedy, a thriller, a period drama, etc.) are clearly identifiable. "If the genre of the film is clear, this helps prepare the ground to sell the film," says Adriana Chiesa, president of Adriana Chiesa Enterprises, an Italian sales company.

A point repeatedly stressed by European sales agents is that they frequently receive packages presented in an unprofessional manner—documents are presented in a scruffy form, are poorly photocopied, and contain many spelling mistakes. Since competition among aspiring producers is intense—many sales agents receive 600 to 700 scripts a year—packages submitted in such a form will not even secure a sales agent's tentative interest.

Given the script's crucial importance in attracting sales agent's interest, it (and its accompanying documents) must be neatly bound and covered. The overall package should be attractive without being ostentatious and embody the highest levels of professional presentation.

(Visual images of the proposed film are considered helpful by some sales agents.)

Providing the right tools to the sales agent is also critical for the subsequent selling the picture to distributors.

■ Preparing to Sell

Many sales agents construct their sales strategy for a picture around one of the three major annual film markets.[2] However, major sales agents usually tie up their film sales in the major territories well in advance of one of these events, using these markets to mop up smaller countries and to gather market intelligence from distributors in key territories. For the smaller sales agents, the markets will be more of a focal point for their selling efforts. For all types of sales agents, the markets will be a forum for discussing forthcoming projects.

The three key markets are the ones held in Cannes in mid-May (during the same period as the film festival), the Mercato Internazionale Film e Documentario (MIFED) in Milan in late October, and the American Film Market (AFM) in Los Angeles in late February. A smaller market, chiefly used by vendors of arthouse films, is held in Berlin in mid-February.

Whether a film's sales strategy hinges on a market or not, certain basic tenets for initially creating distributor interest must be set in motion well before any market. The need to allow sufficient time for this process is paramount.

As has been emphasized above, the international sales industry is relatively small, and personal relationships carry considerable weight. As a result, a sales agent may mention a specific upcoming project to a distributor long before that film is ready to be sold. This will ease the way for the distributor when it comes to the process of actually selling a film. Because each film is a singular event—and any film, in

---

[2] The different ways in which these markets are used is complex and dealt with in Section 4: Markets and Festivals.

theory, has the potential to be a hit–distributors are always eager to learn about new films, and there can be intense competition for certain titles.

Many producers believe that they can do without a sales agent. Although some producers may be able to sell or license their films, it is unlikely that they will have the time, expertise, or strength to fully deliver the films and collect the funds that are due them. What many producers underestimate is the context in which international sales agents work–how through their daily contacts with distributors around the world, they can gauge the temperature of the current buyers market. This gives sales agents not only a vast amount of information about trends and popularity of stars, directors, and genres, but also, perhaps most importantly, an objective perspective on the value of the films they represent, which is something no producer can replicate.

Because of the quality of competition in the marketplace, one of a sales agent's key functions is creating the right marketing strategy to excite distributors. To create a "hot" title, the package presented to buyers should have the right ingredients in terms of script, director, and talent. Just as the method of presentation is very important when a producer pitches a project to a sales agent, the method of presentation is very important when a sales company approaches an international distributor to sell a film. In an increasing number of instances, both European and American independent films may be competing for attention with films produced by the U.S. majors, because the studios sometimes choose to retain only U.S. distribution rights to their films and sell off their foreign rights through international sales agents. In such cases, the studios are able to utilize a sales agent's expertise in assessing the different strengths of each international market. Offloading foreign rights to these companies is often the most effective way of maximizing revenues while also reducing a studio's exposure to production costs.

When a Synopsis Will Do

The sales agent's initial goal is to supply the distributor with the basic facts about the film that is to be sold. This will usually include a synopsis of the storyline or a full script accompanied by information about the track record of the key persons involved (usually the director, the cast, the producer, and, to a lesser degree, the screenwriter). According to Wendy Palmer, Chief Executive Officer of United Artists Films, the ideal length for such a synopsis is about "one page in length. It shouldn't be too long or it won't convey the excitement of the project." In some cases, a sales agent will use an outside writer, such as a journalist, to construct the synopsis. To communicate some of a film's distinctive flavor and whip up the distributors' interest in hearing more about the project (so that they will ask to read the script), some sales agents prefer to speak to distributors prior to sending out the synopsis.

Some sales companies will not send out a synopsis, preferring to start with the full-length screenplay, which is sent to selected buyers in the major territories. The script will usually be accompanied by details of the U.S. distribution deal, which, if in place, should increase the value of the film. If a budget for the film has been drawn up, some financial details may also be released, but the sales company's first objective is to get people excited by the story and the script itself.

The Importance of the U.S. Deal

Securing a U.S. deal is a critical element in ensuring a reasonable chance of raising funds for a film. Since the U.S. is the largest homogenous marketplace in the world, selling U.S. rights will enormously enhance a picture's earning potential, particularly if it's acquired by a company such as Miramax, October Films, or PolyGram, all of which have reputations for turning specialized films into box-office hits. (Miramax achieved $62.5 million in North America for *The Crying Game* and $107 million for *Pulp Fiction*, October recorded a gross box-office of $13 million for *Secrets and Lies*, and PolyGram did $52.7 million on *Four Weddings and a Funeral.*)

For a film's potential foreign buyers, information about its U.S. deal is important because it indicates the level of exposure that the film should receive. By virtue of its size, the U.S. market ensures that most films receive some media visibility when they are released. If a film is a success in the U.S. (not to mention the publicity surrounding an

Academy Award nomination or a Golden Globe win), foreign distributors will hope that that success will create a buzz that will percolate through to other countries.

"Since the U.S. is the largest homogeneous marketplace in the world, selling U.S. rights will enormously enhance a picture's earning potential."

A U.S. deal can also confer credibility on a film, particularly in cases where the picture involves relatively unknown talent. The fact that a film has a U.S. distribution deal is a valuable vote of confidence in the project, because it is made by buyers in the world's most important—and probably most lucrative—market. This assumes, of course, that the film is released and well-received in the U.S. before its release in other territories. In cases where a film performs poorly in the U.S., foreign distributors may experience a negative effect from its high visibility, since bad publicity may travel in advance of the film and deter customers in other territories.

While certain well-connected producers may wish to approach U.S. sources themselves, they would be well advised to employ an experienced film lawyer because distribution contracts are notoriously lengthy and complicated.

MARKETS AND FESTIVALS

Section **4**

The major markets and festivals are crucial dates in the diaries of film sales and marketing executives. Depending on the stage of a film's production process (i.e., preproduction, shooting, postproduction, or completed), a different strategy will be devised for each market and festival. In broad terms, the most important factor determining the approach to a specific event is whether it is a market or a festival, since the two events are quite different in nature.

As discussed in the previous section, the three most important film markets are Cannes in mid-May (during the same period as the film festival), MIFED held in Milan in late October, and the American Film Market (AFM) in Los Angeles in late February. A smaller market held during the Ber-

> *"The atmosphere at these events is similar to that of a bazaar."*

lin Film Festival in mid-February is primarily used for the sales of arthouse films. (See the accompanying chart of major events in the international film calendar.)

At the three most important film markets, most of the major international sales agents will hire office space from where they will conduct business with the hundreds of film distributors who attend to buy films. The atmosphere at these events is similar to that of a bazaar.

Few festivals, with the exception of Cannes and Berlin, incorporate an official film market. The primary aim of a festival is to showcase films for the benefit of the press and the public. However, many distributors will often attend selected festivals to see films that they are considering buying and to talk to any visiting sales agents and producers.

To maximize the value of film markets, sales companies must plan their market campaigns well in advance and prepare certain key materials that will be used to attract the attention of distributors, the trade press, and, in the case of Cannes, the consumer press. As is stressed throughout this book, allocating the required time and resources for planning and executing all aspects of a marketing campaign is a critical but often under-valued means of helping to ensure success. This section will examine the strategies and tools to be used under different circumstances, and demonstrate how producers can maximize the value of such events.

Calendar of Major Events in the Film Year

JANUARY

Palm Springs International Film Festival (California, USA)
11 days early Jan
Tel: 1-619/328.34.56.
Sundance Film Festival (Park City, USA)
11 days
Tel: 1-801/328-34.56.
Brussels International Film Festival (Belgium)
10 days mid Jan
Tel: 32-2/218.10.55.
Rotterdam Film Festival (Netherlands)
12 days end Jan
Tel: 310-10/411.80.80.

Awards:
Golden Globes
(Hollywood
Foreign Press
Association
Awards)

FEBRUARY

Göteborg Film Festival (Sweden)
10 days early Feb
Tel: 46-31/41.05.46
Monte Carlo International TV Festival and Market (Monaco)
7 days early Feb
Tel: 33/93.30.49.44.
Berlin International Film Festival (Germany)
12 days mid Feb
Tel: 49-30/254.892.25.

Nominations:
BAFTA (UK)
Cesars (France)
Goyas (Spain)
Oscars (Usa)

AFM **American Film Market** (Los Angeles, USA)
10 days end Feb
Tel: 1-310/447.15.55.

MARCH

NATO/Showest Convention for U.S. distributors, exhibitors
(Las Vegas, USA)
4 days early March
Tel: 1-310/657.77.24

Awards:
BAFTA
Cesars
Goyas
Oscars

APRIL

Istanbul International Film Festival (Turkey)
16 days early April
Tel: 90-1/260.45.33.
MIP-TV International TV & Video Market (Cannes, France)
6 days mid April
Tel: 33-1/44.34.44.44

MAY

CANNES **Cannes International Film Festival
and Market** (France)
12 days mid May
Tel: - Official selection : 33-1/42.66.92.20.
       - Director's Fortnight: 33-1/45.61.01.66.
       - Critics Week: 33-1/45.75.68.27.
       - International Film Market: 33-1/44.13.40.40.

JUNE

Midnight Sun Film Festival (Sodankylä, Finland)
5 days
Tel: 358-96/.93.21.008.
Troia International Film Festival (Portugal)
10 days early June
Tel: 351-65/441.21.
Cinema Expo International (Brussels, Belgium)
4 days end June
Tel: 32-2/478.31.97.
Munich Film Festival (Germany)
7 days end June
Tel: 49-89/381.90.40.
Mysfest Film Festival (Cattolica, Italy)
8 days end June
Tel: 39-54/967.802.

Awards:
David Di
Donatello (Italy)

JULY

Karlovy Vary International Film Festival (Czech Republic)
Tel: 42-27.58.14.23.
Moscow International Film Festival (Russia)
Biannual event
12 days early July
Tel: 7-095/297.76.45.
Taormina Film Festival (Italy)
7 days end July
Tel: 39-6/322.64.13.

AUGUST

Locarno International Film Festival (Switzerland)
11 days early August
Tel: 41-93/310.232.
Edinburgh International Film Festival (U.K.)
16 days mid August
Tel: 44-31/228.40.51.
Haugesund Film Festival (Norway)
7 days end August
Tel: 47-4/734.300.
Montreal World Film Festival (Canada)
12 days end August
Tel: 1-514/933.96.99.

SEPTEMBER

Deauville US Film Festival (France) 10 days early Sept
Tel: 33-1/46.40.55.00.
Telluride Film Festival (USA) 4 days early Sept
Tel: 1-603/643.12.55.
Toronto Festival of Festivals (Canada) 10 days
Tel: 1-416/967.73.71.
Venice International Film Festival (Italy) 12 days early Sept
Tel: 39-41/52.18.711.
San Sebastian International Film Festival (Spain)
10 days mid Sept. Tel: 34-43/481.212.
Dutch Film Days (Utrecht, Netherlands) 10 days end Sept
Tel: 31-30/32.26.84.
IFFM International Feature Film Market (USA) 9 days end Sept
Tel: 1-212/243.77.77.
Tokyo International Film Festival and Market (Japan)
11 days end Sept
Tel: 81-3/35.63.63.05.

OCTOBER

New York Film Festival (USA) 17 days early Oct
Tel: 1-212/875.56.10.
Vancouver International Film Festival (Canada)
17 days early Oct
Tel: 1-604/685.02.60.
Ghent International Film Festival of Flanders (Belgium)
12 days mid Oct
Tel: 32-9/221.89.46.
MIPCOM International TV and video market (Cannes, France)
5 days mid Oct
Tel: 33-1/44.34.44.44.

MIFED

MIFED International Film Market
(Milan, Italy) 6 days end Oct
Tel: 39-2/48.01.29.12.
Valladollid International Film Festival (Spain)
9 days end Oct
Tel: 34-83/305.700

NOVEMBER

London Film Festival (U.K.)
18 days early Nov
Tel: 44-71/815.13.25
Sarasota French Film Festival (Florida, USA)
6 days mid Nov
Tel: 1-813/351.90.10

DECEMBER

Cairo International Film Festival (Egypt)
10 days early Dec
Tel: 202/393.89.79.
Havana International Film Festival (Cuba)
late Dec
Tel: 53-7/34.400.

Awards:
Felix (Best
European films of
the year)

Working the Markets

The larger sales companies tend to use film markets for informing distributors of what is in the pipeline and updating their knowledge of trends in the key territories. Although sales agents will maintain constant contact with international distributors throughout the year, markets present an opportunity to meet face-to-face with a large number of people in a relatively short space of time.

If a large sales company is pre-selling a picture, most of the deals for the larger territories will have been completed by the time the company arrives at the market. Sales agent from these companies will use the market to try to mop up sales on unsold territories, which are usually the smaller territories or those that are more difficult to pre-sell. (Pre-sales are most common in such large territories as the U.K., Germany, Italy, Spain, and France, since most of these territories have very competitive distribution sectors and strong television industries that, with theatrical distributors, can commit considerable sums to acquiring rights.)

For the smaller sales companies, the markets are used for more of a sales push, since the ingredients of the specialized films that they tend to handle are often not strong enough to be pre-sold on the basis of telephone conversations and script mailings. Sales agents from these companies will need to have face-to-face conversations with potential buyers, and will often screen completed films in an effort to incite interest.

When sales agents first acquire the rights to sell a particular picture, they will analyze how the proposed schedule for that film's preproduction, production, and postproduction ties in with the schedules of the various film markets. (See Lifestages of a Film.) With the goal of building a momentum or a buzz around the picture, they will then draw up a strategy for approaching each event, which will be timed to peak when the picture is first screened at a market. The nature of this strategy will be a crucial means of boosting sales.

At the first film market, the sales agent's aim will usually be to generate an initial sense of excitement around the project, based on such elements in the film as the likely cast, the director, or the storyline. This will form a prelude to a full-blooded sales campaign, which is likely to start at the second market.

Even before a market opens, sales agents will talk to distributors about forthcoming films to ensure that distributors arrive at a market with some prior knowledge of a project.

■ Key Marketing Tools at the First Market

The marketing tools used during the first market will continue to be used at subsequent markets, but they will usually be augmented by other materials. The main elements are as follows:

The Shooting Script

The shooting script is the marketing-package element that is most likely to hook potential buyers. Most distributors will wish to see this script, particularly if they are being asked to put up relatively large sums of money for the picture. Distributors may wish to take the script away and read it on their return home, enabling them to make a considered decision about the picture. If possible, the script should be sent out to key buyers six to eight weeks before a market. This practice allows distributors sufficient time to read it and, in turn, makes the market meetings more effective, since the sales agent will be dealing with distributors who have read the script and will base their offers accordingly.

> *" The script should be sent out to key buyers six to eight weeks before a market. "*

Lifestages of a Film

The lifestages of a film can be broken down into six main sections which are detailed below. This breakdown is intended to act as a guide to the various stages which a film may pass through, although the pattern may vary for each individual film, and not all stages may be applicable. A different marketing strategy will be used at each step. Steps one to four deal with selling the film to the industry; step five deals with theatrical distribution and step six with ancillary rights.

How and when to implement the marketing plan will depend on the type of film being made, what is perceived to be the optimum time to initiate and conclude sales and, of course, the actual response to the film as it is being made and when it is completed.

1 — PREPRODUCTION

Idea (existing/adaptation)

Development

Treatment

Script (drafts)

Financing

Possible pre-sales

Positioning elements
— Introduction to targeted buyers/distributors
— Introduction to general trade (e.g. exhibitors, festivals etc)
— Through trade press announcements, industry events

Preliminary image

2 — PRODUCTION

Further financing

Pre-sales to commence (script and package elements to key buyers)

Introduction to further buyers

Preliminary image (if not commenced in preproduction stage)

Stills, footage, showreel may be produced to assist in sales

3 — POSTPRODUCTION

Showreel (if not produced above)

Trailer (commence production of)

Visual or poster

Festival selections

Pre-sales based on above to continue and/or building word of mouth

4 — COMPLETED

Screening completed film

Festival, market, or other platform

Positioning to industry and public
— Distributors, response
— Critics, response
— Refine image, trailer

Prepare to deliver to distribution

5 — IN DISTRIBUTION MARKETING TO THE PUBLIC/COMPLETE SALES

Festival platform to consider

Release in its domestic territory;

What effect will it have on other territories, especially those not yet sold?

Release in other European territories

In the U.S.

Marketing parameters
— Audience/critics, reaction
— Festival response
— Other films' performance
— Cast's performance in other films

6 — OTHER MEDIA

How will theatrical release affect eventual sale to ancillary markets, video, television?

If already sold, how will theatrical release affect video revenue (i.e. number of videos rented or sold) and value to future television sales?

The Synopsis

Both a short and a long synopsis of the film will be useful for buyers who are at a market for just a few days and, therefore, do not have time to read an entire script. Also, a full script won't always be available for markets—so being armed with a synopsis would be essential in such a case.

Stills, Filmographies, and Background Information

Filmographies and biographical information on the leading cast and crew members can be very effective tools in helping a sales effort. (This material can be supplied by either the production company or the agents representing the individuals concerned.) But, unfortunately, such materials are too often neglected. Such neglect may damage a film's chances of success because these materials will help a buyer evaluate a project based on the caliber, pedigree, and previous box-office results of its key actors, director, and other personnel. This information may be supported by color or black-and-white stills of the cast, especially in the case of new talent, because stills will help distributors visualize a film and its screen characters. (Even stills available from an actor's agent can be helpful.)

Publicity and Press

Publicity will play a crucial role in informing the industry and the press about a film when it is first launched at a market. Coordinating advertising, editorial, and promotional events should not be underestimated. Specialist public relations and marketing companies should be engaged to create a strong image and maximize the potential of any film.

Publicity will be handled by either a sales agent's in-house marketing person or an outside publicity company. Companies that specialize in film publicity exist in the major territories. Such companies will usually be hired by the producer, who will make decisions in conjunction with the sales agent. If there is no sales agent or publicity company attached, the responsibility for press and publicity would then fall to the producer.

A publicity company's first task is to ensure that the industry is aware that a film is going to be made. This will be achieved by issuing a press release that will include details about the director and key cast members and a brief summary of the storyline. This is often done by the unit publicist, an individual attached to the shoot to handle press and publicity.

For larger pictures, information about the U.S. distribution deal (if any) may also be included in this release. If this deal occurs at the same time as a market, then a more detailed release will be circulated to all trade press attending the market for inclusion in their daily publications. The unit publicist's goal is to maximize a film's media coverage, to make the public aware of a film at an early stage, and to interest potential distributors.

In addition to issuing a press release, a publicist may also organize a press conference, perhaps on the set or, if practical, at nearby film festival or market at which the trade and selected consumer press will be invited to meet and question the film's stars and director. The goal of this conference is to generate early press coverage, which will help to interest distributors in the film. In view of the fierce competition for the press' attention, one must have a strong hook with which to attract the media, otherwise this event will reflect badly on the film, and be costly as well.

Such press conferences are a particular feature of Cannes, where a huge number of representatives of both the consumer and the trade press from around the world are gathered. Although much of their attention is focused on the completed films showing at the festival, the mere presence of so many journalists and photographers can offer ample scope for the sales agent to secure coverage of films that are in their earliest stages of development. The number of accredited press at Cannes is generally about 3,500, including fifty to sixty television crews.

At the American Film Market (AFM) and MIFED, the press presence is largely confined to journalists from the trade publications, because these two markets are not accompanied by a festival where completed films are shown in competition with each other. At the AFM, distributors will occasionally host celebrity receptions to help launch a film, but very few press events occur at MIFED.

Announcing Ad

Depending on one's marketing budget, an "announcing" ad for a film may be placed in the trade magazines to complement a film's first-market press release. This ad allows one to have control of the information and image presented and guarantees the coverage that a press release may not generate.

As previously indicated, the three main international trade papers are *Variety, Screen International,* and *The Hollywood Reporter.*[1] *Moving Pictures International* also produces a daily edition during the major film markets. These publications are supplemented by such publications as *Le Film Français,* a French trade publication, *Blickpunkt Film* in Germany, *Cinema d'Oggi* in Italy, and a number of other trades in different countries. During the three main film markets, some or all of these publications publish daily editions that are circulated at the markets, and in which sales agents frequently advertise their films.

Trade Listings

Once a film has been unveiled, a sales agent will include it in the trade listings published in the film trades' "bumper" issues, which appear in advance of each market. A trade listings is a comprehensive, alphabetical list of the sales agents who will be attending a particular market, together with brief details of the films they will be selling at the market.

The value of free publicity, such as trade listings, is often underestimated. At Cannes, for example, there is no official guide to all the

---

[1] *Variety* and *The Hollywood Reporter* publish daily editions in Los Angeles, Monday through Friday. *Variety* also publishes a daily edition in New York. Both *Variety* and *The Hollywood Reporter* publish weekly international editions that are circulated around the world. *Screen International* is published in the U.K. on a weekly basis and circulated around the world.

films on offer at the market, so the trade papers offer the distributors invaluable information about what's being sold. Bumper

" The value of free publicity, such as trade listings, is often underestimated. "

issues will also be widely consulted at both MIFED and AFM, although official information about the films being offered for sale is more readily available at these two markets.

Keeping in Touch

From the first market to the second market, a sales agent must maintain constant communication with a film's potential buyers, because it may take two or three markets to convince a buyer to put up money for a film.

The publicity company or sales agent will usually attach a unit publicist to a production once it starts shooting. This publicist will seek to generate location reports in mainstream magazines and newspapers, as well as in the trade press, usually focusing on a certain aspect of the film, such as a certain star or director, as a hook to interest the media. In other cases, topical or unusual subject matter may be used to incite press coverage.

Another technique employed by publicists is to close a set or restrict entry to it to a few selected journalists. This is done in the hope that an atmosphere of intrigue and heightened expectation will be generated among the public during the run-up to the film's release. This strategy is particularly suited to films that involve unusual subject matter or have a novel plot thrust. The goal is to focus the public's interest on those elements that most sharply distinguish the film from its competition.

■ Key Marketing Tools at the Second Market

A sales campaign will usually start in earnest at the second market, although it will probably not peak until the film receives its market screening, which may not occur until the project has its third, or even fourth, market outing. At the second market, a sales agent will use an additional set of tools to market a picture to distributors, especially if some footage of the film is already available. However, some of the materials used at earlier stages of the marketing process, such as the script, will be used here again.

The first two or three days of the second market will often be spent distributing such materials as synopses and stills to potential buyers and setting up meetings for the third or fourth day of the market, when deals can be negotiated. As a result of those meetings, the sales agent will hope to receive a number of firm offers on a picture and, if the sum offered is acceptable, close the deal.

Delivery Date

If a film is shooting or in postproduction, knowing the likely date when it will be delivered is essential for all concerned. This information will help distributors decide how a film might fit into their likely release schedule (e.g., a summer film, a holiday film, a film tied to school dates) and, should there be any delay in postproduction, allow sales agents sufficient time to adjust their marketing schedule, in particular the date of the completed film's first screening.

The Office Display

Office displays—which feature posters, stills, blow-ups from the film, and images specially designed to give a conceptual feel for the film— are crucial marketing tools at this stage. Since film is a visual medium, these items will implant an image of the film in the minds of its potential distributors and help the film stand out from its among competitors at the market.

The Poster

The poster, also known as a one-sheet or key art, will be based on those elements that the sales agent feels are the film's key selling points. The most common format used for posters is 27 inches x 40 inches (707mm x 1000mm).

At this stage of the marketing process, the poster is often a simple blow-up of a photograph accompanied by a strong title style and credit block, which gives distributors a more concrete idea of the film's genre or style and provides them with ideas about how they might sell the film to the public. However, the photograph used at this point in the poster's development is not necessarily the image that will be used in the final campaign for the film.

The sales agent will commission a design company to produce a design based on the film's key elements. In many cases, the designer will be given as little as two weeks to prepare a poster for a market. Such a short design period is sometimes the result of problems that are beyond the control of the sales agent (e.g., securing approval on paid advertising credits or getting rights to use certain stills can often take much longer than expected).

If the sales agent doesn't commission the poster within a reasonable time frame, there may be insufficient time to create an attractive image and certain suppliers contracted by the poster company, the printers, for example, may have to be paid rush fees. As a result, costs will rise while quality will suffer. Then, when sales agents come to sell the project at a market, they may rapidly discover that a poor poster results in a poor level of sales. Therefore, allowing enough time for the creation of an effective sales poster or brochure is vital. It cannot be stressed enough that a film's first image makes an important statement and impact on potential buyers. If a film's poster is weak, the film will face a disadvantage when competing with the enormous number of other pictures in the marketplace.

Stills

Stills, which may be packaged in books to be shown to visiting distributors, are an important part of the office display. For films that have begun production, stills are a vital marketing tool because they are a highly effective means of conveying a picture's visual style and of highlighting key cast members. Since just two or three visual images from a film may be used repeatedly to promote the film around the world, everything possible must be done to ensure that these photographs are as effective as possible.

Therefore, ensuring that a photographer is on the set while the film is shooting is vital. A photographer who is attached to a film throughout most or all of its shoot is known as the unit photographer. (Where budgets are low, a freelance photographer should be hired for just a few days to cover a picture's key scenes.)

Increasingly, many sales agents and producers hire photographic agencies to take stills. At the outset of the production, clarifying who owns the copyright to the stills (and their negatives) is important. Some agencies give reduced fees for covering a shoot in return for rights to certain stills. Unless properly agreed, this can pose problems when distributors request certain stills and discover that they may have to pay for something to which they thought they had free access.

> **" All photographers should be properly briefed by the producer on the key scenes that they need to cover. "**

All photographers should be properly briefed by the producer on the key scenes that they need to cover. They should also be made to feel welcome on the set and treated like a member of the crew, so that they have the best possible opportunities to take first-class photographs. In many cases, the director will see the on-set shooting of stills as an intrusion. Therefore, the producer must ensure that the unit photographer is allowed to do his or her job properly and that everyone is aware of the importance of the photographs. If this is not done, the marketing campaign for the film may be adversely affected and the performance of the film may therefore suffer once it is released.

"To secure the best possible images of the cast, it may be necessary to set aside a day that is dedicated to photographs."

To secure the best possible images of the cast, it may be necessary to set aside a day that is dedicated to photographs. Stills taken at the location or studio where the film is shooting, since they will usually feature the actors in character, are generally much more effective than shots made of key cast members at a later stage. Conducting stills photography at this point will also be cheaper because most of the cast are in one place. The cost of shooting stills when the film is finished may be as much as five times higher than it would be while the film is in production.

If a film doesn't feature well-known stars, it will be particularly important to shoot the stills while the film is shooting, since individual photographs of the stars taken later won't have much appeal to the media. In such cases, the role of the stills as a marketing tool will be to convey the film's mood rather than to sell the picture based on its leading actors.

Sales companies will often prepare books containing as many as fifty stills. In such cases, it is vital that the stills are held back until the right moment–otherwise their publicity value will be wasted. For instance, some producers will sell their stills to photographic agencies that will syndicate sales of them to magazines around the world. But these agencies often fail to ensure that the stills appear at the most effective time for publicizing a film–they may sell the photographs to a national magazines for publication six months before the film is released in that territory. As a consequence, when the film is about to be released, the publications that have already published the photographs will refuse to republish them, and a major opportunity to publicize the film has been lost.

The Showreel

If some footage of the film has already been shot, the sales agent will often want to cut a five- to fifteen-minute showreel. In effect, a showreel is the film's précis. As such, it offers a more comprehensive taste of the film than a trailer. Because the film may still be incomplete, the showreel's footage may be taken from a rough cut and accompanied by a temporary music track. The showreel may be put together either on film (which is likely to cost between $18,600 to $25,000, largely due to the high laboratory costs) or on video (which costs between $7,500 and $12,000). Showreels are specialist tools that should be assembled by specialist companies that have a knowledge of what is required. Cutting a showreel is very different from cutting a feature or even a trailer.

Rough Cut of the Trailer

A rough cut of a film's trailer may also be shown to potential buyers. It gives distributors a sense of how the film will or can be marketed and helps reinforce the showreel's impact by singling out some of the film's particularly dramatic moments and imparting a sense of the film's overall tone. Such a trailer may be as short as thirty seconds, but in most cases, it will last two to three minutes. If cut on high-quality videotape, it will usually cost around $10,000 to $15,000.

The Brochure

For some films, sales companies will create a brochure to promote the films to both distributors and the trade press. However, brochures are costly and, consequently, will only be used where judged to be particularly effective. Also, access to materials that have been approved by the leading cast members can be difficult to obtain. Frequently, the stars' agents, concerned that their clients get sufficient prominence in promotional materials, require lengthy negotiations before the use of certain photographs will be permitted.

The cover of the film's brochure, which will usually be printed on a heavy paper stock to lend weight and texture to the document, will often be a version of the film's poster art. Inside, the brochure will usually contain the film's synopsis, designed to arouse the interest of buyers, and information about the track record of the director, the principal cast, and, in some cases, the producer. A selection of stills will accompany the text. The brochure's overall length will depend on the film's budget, but it will usually run from eight to thirty-two pages.

Some sales companies choose to wait until after the film has been completed before they work on its brochure. In so doing, the brochure will reflect the fully developed visual nuances of the final film. Therefore, it will have a longer shelf life and be more cost effective.

For such an event as Cannes, as many as 1,500 to 2,000 different brochures will be created, each of which may have cost between $12,000 and $30,000, depending on production values and the use of color. Such costs mean that, in most cases, only larger films will be able to afford elaborate brochures.

After the second market, the sales agent will maintain regular contact with distributors so that they are appraised of all developments concerning the picture. By the time of the third or the fourth market, the film will usually be ready for screening in its entirety. At this stage in its life, it may also be entered for screening at a film festival.

■ Key Marketing Tools at the Third Market

Trade Advertising

At the third market, the goal of trade advertising is to maximize a picture's visibility. To ensure that larger pictures have a high profile, sales companies will often take out double-page advertising spreads. These advertisements will usually be run in the bumper editions of the trades and in the daily market issues. If the budget is large enough, this advertising may run over several days, culminating on the day the film is to receive its market screening.

One way of ensuring a film's high visibility is to take out a prime-position—a frontcover, a backcover, or an early right-hand page—trade ad. Since every film is competing with hundreds of others for the attention of potential buyers, securing the best possible advertising (within the marketing budget's constraints) is important. Prime ad space in the trade papers will often need to be booked in advance of the market. Ad costs can range from $500 for a quarter-page black-and-white to $10,500 for a full page in full color. Premium positions usually cost up to twenty-five percent extra. Cost-effective marketing calls for rigorous negotiation with the trade papers because advertising is one of the major costs in selling a film to the international distribution community.

For pictures in which such elements as the story, the cast, or the director have already proved strongly intriguing to distributors, pursuing a more low-key promotional approach that targets only a few selected buyers may be preferable. In certain instances, an aura of exclusivity may be built around a film by reducing its advertising volume and concentrating on targeted buyers and direct mail or offering "invite only" passes to the first screening of the completed film.

Market Screenings

Once a film is completed, the task of the sales agent handling it is to complete sales on unsold territories, which will often include many of the smaller countries around the world.

A market screening acts as a film's showcase. For the sales agent, the object of a market screening is to persuade distributors to buy a film at the highest possible price. On the basis of this screening, those distributors who have not yet committed to a film will decide whether to buy it—and at what price.

The market screening will be booked in advance by the sales agent, either through the market organizers or directly with an individual cinema. In the case of Cannes, market screenings are held in the Palais des Festivals and in the city's public cinemas, which are given over to the festival for the duration of the event. At MIFED, screenings will be held in cinemas located inside the exhibition hall, the Fiera Internazionale di Milano. At the AFM, screenings will usually be held at one of the many cinema complexes in the Santa Monica area of the host city, Los Angeles.

> *"Ideally, the market screening should be held somewhere around the middle of the market. This will allow the sales agent time to create a buzz prior to the screening."*

Ideally, the market screening should be held somewhere around the middle of the market. This will allow the sales agent time to create a buzz prior to the screening. The time between the screening and the end of the market will then be used to close deals with various distributors.

As with cost-effective and well-placed trade advertising, knowing when and where to screen a film at a market or a festival–particularly for its first screening–requires a clear strategy. Buyers have been waiting to see the film since its early days of production, and with hundreds of films screening and perhaps thousands of dollars being spent on promotion and advertising, selecting the right day, the right time, and the right cinema for the screening is

> *"Selecting the right day, the right time, and the right cinema for the screening is of paramount importance."*

of paramount importance. Only through close discussion with market/festival organizers, proper completion of a screening application, and a thorough knowledge of how each market works, can this crucial step be successfully achieved.

In most cases, the picture will be given more than one market screening, although the sales agent may limit the number of screenings in the hope of creating a sense of exclusivity around the project. Since the community of distributors is small, it should be possible to reach the most important buyers with two or three screenings, some of which take place before the official market to give the more favored

Schedule for First Day of MIFED (1998)

NOVEMBER 1 — sunday

HALL 8 · MEZZANINE (2nd/top floor) · HALL C3 (1st Floor)

TIME	PURICELLI	LEONARDO	700	19	20	21	22	23	24
9.30	WIGGLES MOVIE, THE / BEYOND FILMS LIMITED	BASE, THE / AMERICAN WORLD PICTURES		BESAME MUCHO (Kiss me more) / ADRIANA CHIESA ENTERPRISES		RUN LOLA RUN / BAVARIA FILM INTERNATIONAL	TERRA NOVA / FORTISSIMO FILM SALES	AND NOW YOU'RE DEAD / GOLDEN HARVEST	THREE SEASONS / GOOD MACHINE
11.30	RUSH HOUR / NEW LINE CINEMA	YOU CAN THANK ME LATER / DANEHIP ENTERTAINMENT	JUSTICE / INTERLIGHT PICTURES	ACTS OF JUSTICE (Per tutto il tempo che ci resta) / ADRIANA CHIESA ENTERPRISES		NIGHT TIME (Sieben Monde) / CINEPOOL	TORRENTE, EL BRAZO TONTO (Torrente, the dumb arm of the law) / LOLAFILMS/CLT-UFA INTERNATIONAL	ANOTHER DAY IN PARADISE / KATHY MORGAN INTERNATIONAL	BRIDE OF CHUCKY / GOOD MACHINE
13.30	LIVING OUT LOUD / NEW LINE CINEMA	SIBERIA / FILM FOUR INTERNATIONAL	G-2 / S ENTERTAINMENT	IL SIGNOR QUINDICIPALLE / ADRIANA CHIESA ENTERPRISES		I WONDER WHO'S KISSING YOU NOW? / BV INTERNATIONAL	FESTEN-Dogme 1 / WORLD SALES CHRISTA SAREDI	CLOWN AT MIDNIGHT, THE / BLUE RIDER INTERNATIONAL	DON'T GO BREAKIN' MY HEART / CURB ENTERTAINMENT
15.30	DEAR CLAUDIA / BEYOND FILMS LIMITED	DARKNESS FALLS / VINE INTERNATIONAL	ELIZABETH / POLYGRAM FILM (15.20)	23 / BAVARIA FILM INTERNATIONAL	LANI LOA / LE STUDIO CANAL+	FRONTLINE / SHOWCASE ENTERTAINMENT		WISDOM OF CROCODILES, THE / GOLDWYN FILMS	IF...DOG...RUBBIT / FRANCHISE PICTURES
17.30	EVERYBODY LOVES SUNSHINE / IAC FILM	THICK AS THIEVES / MOONSTONE ENTERTAINMENT	HI-LO COUNTRY / POLYGRAM FILM	ESMERALDA COMES BY NIGHT / OVERSEAS FILMGROUP	KANZO SENSEI / LE STUDIO CANAL+	TONI / FRANCE TELEVISION DISTRIBUTION	WINDHORSE / SCENERIES INTERNATIONAL	BLACK CAT WHITE CAT / GOLDWYN FILMS	20 DATES / FRANCHISE PICTURES
19.30	LA NINA DE TUS OJOS (Girl of your Dreams) / VINE INTERNATIONAL	CLAIRE DOLAN / MK2 DIFFUSION			WOUNDS, THE / LE STUDIO CANAL+ (19.40)	FEUERREITER / PROGRESS FILM		BITTERSWEET / KANDICE KING PRODUCTIONS	MASCARA / RGH/LIONS SHARE PICTURES

RIDOTTO (Top Floor)

TIME	1	2	3	4	5	6	8	9	10
9.30	HIDDEN AGENDA / ALLIANCE/LE MONDE		LATE AUGUST, EARLY SEPTEMBER / UGC INTERNATIONAL			CONVERGENCE / WHITE ROCK FILM INTERNATIONAL		ELEVENTH CHILD, THE / M6 DROITS AUDIOVISUELS	
11.30	PERPETRATORS OF THE CRIME / MOTION INTERNATIONAL	NORTH END, THE / ARTHUR KANANACK & ASSOCIATES	LET'S TALK ABOUT SEX / TF1 INTERNATIONAL	PRAISE / SOUTHERN STAR FILM SALES	FALCONE / HBO ENTERPRISES	ONE HELL OF A GUY / ATMOSPHERE ENTERTAINMENT	DENTIST 2, THE / TRIMARK PICTURES	DESERT THUNDER / CINETEL FILMS	L'ECOLE DE LA CHAIR (The school of flesh) / FLACH PYRAMIDE INTERNATIONAL
13.30	DEAD LETTER OFFICE / SOUTHERN STAR FILM SALES	RETURN TO SAVAGE BEACH / ARTHUR KANANACK & ASSOCIATES	POWDER KEG, THE (Bume Baruta) / UGC INTERNATIONAL	TOP OF THE FOOD CHAIN / VICTOR FILM	LOVE KILLS / TRIDENT RELEASING	CHARITY BIZNESS / TF1 INTERNATIONAL	AMERICAN CUISINE / CAPITOL FILMS	ORPHANS / BEYOND FILMS LIMITED	GIRL NEXT DOOR, ? / STORM ENTERTAINMENT
15.30	IN THE WINTER DARK / SOUTHERN STAR FILM SALES	LOS ANOS BARBAROS / SOGEPAQ INTERNATIONAL	LES KIDNAPPEURS / UGC INTERNATIONAL	YOU ALONE CAN'T SEE / NIKKATSU CORPORATION	BEDROOMS & HALLWAYS / PANDORA CINEMA	GENERAL, THE / J & M ENTERTAINMENT (15.20)	ANGEL'S DANCE / PROMARK ENTERTAINMENT GROUP	COPPIA OMICIDA (Love & Kill) / FILMEXPORT GROUP	I STAND ALONE (Seul contre tous) / CELLULOID DREAM
17.30	NO / ALLIANCE/LE MONDE	BLOODSPORT:THE DARK KUMITE / F.M. ENTERTAINMENT	DIE SIEBTELBAUERN (The Inheritors) / FORTISSIMO FILM SALES	TRAIN DE VIE (Train of Life) / AB INTERNATIONAL	STORMRIDERS, THE / GOLDEN HARVEST	VIGO - PASSION FOR LIFE / FILM FOUR INTERNATIONAL	SECRET PACT,THE / SABAN INTERNATIONAL	PER AMORE SOLO PER AMORE (For love only for love) / FILMEXPORT GROUP	ICE RINK, THE (La Patinoire) / FILMS DISTRIBUTION
19.30	JACK AND JILL / ALLIANCE/LE MONDE	OTHER CONQUEST, THE / STORM ENTERTAINMENT	VOLEUR DE VIE / TF1 INTERNATIONAL	HERMES / SCENERIES INTERNATIONAL	NOT EVEN THE TREES / SEAGAL-NASSO DISTRIBUTION	MARTHA - MEET FRANK, DANIEL AND LAURENCE / FILM FOUR INTERNATIONAL	BILLY'S HOLLYWOOD SCREEN KISS / TRIMARK PICTURES		J'AIMERAIS PAS CREVER UN DIMANCHE / FLACH PYRAMIDE INTERNATIONAL

Schedule for First Day of MIFED (1998) (cont.)

HALL D4. (2nd Floor)

MARCONI	VENEZIA	LUMIERE	7	
	LA WITHOUT A MAP THE SALES COMPANY			NOVEMBER 1
BOY MEETS GIRL BEYOND FILMS LIMITED	DANCE,THE THE SALES COMPANY	ACAO ENTRE AMIGOS (Friendly Fire) NORTH AND SOUTH FILM	FIGLI DI ANNIBALE INTRA FILMS	11.30
TAXMAN KUSHNER-LOCKE CO.	TICHBORNE CLAIMANT, THE THE SALES COMPANY	I WOKE UP EARLY THE DAY I DIED CINEQUANON PICTURES	MIRAMAX PROMO REEL MIRAMAX INTERNATIONAL HALLOWEEN H20 MIRAMAX INTERNATIONAL	13.30 13.55
JACOB TWO TWO MEETS THE HOODED FANG NORTH AND SOUTH FILM	SOUTHERN CROSS FRIES FILM GROUP	DOG PARK LIONS GATE FILMS	LITTLE VOICE MIRAMAX INTERNATIONAL	15.30
PHANTOM OF THE OPERA, THE ADRIANA CHIESA ENTERPRISES	HURRAH INTERMEDIA	BVFS FILM BY INVITATION ONLY	ROUNDERS MIRAMAX INTERNATIONAL	17.30
COHEN V. ROSI BUENA VISTA FILM SALES	MERCHANTS OF VENLS AMAZING MOVIES	BULLET BALLET GOLD VIEW CO.	VIG LIONS GATE FILMS	19.30

Sunday

11	12	13	14	15	CAMPERIO HALL 8 VIDEO CASSETTE
		PLANET OF JUNIOR BROWN MYRIAD PICTURES	FINDING GRACELAND LARGO ENTERTAINMENT		
ECCO FATTO (That's it) RAI TRADE	SOMBRE CELLULOID DREAMS	ALL NEW ADVENTURES OF LAUREL & HARDY, THE-FOR LOVE OR MUMMY COAST ENTERTAINMENT	SIX-STRING SAMURAI OVERSEAS FILMGROUP	CADILLAC PORTMAN ENTERTAINMENT	FOOTSTEPS AMCO ENTERTAINMENT
L'ESTATE DI DAVIDE (David's summer) RAI TRADE	24 HOUR WOMAN, THE THE SHOOTING GALLERY	REBIRTH OF MOTHRA II MOTION PICTURE PROD.ASS.OF JAPAN	A TRUE MOB STORY CHINA STAR ENTERTAINMENT	BROWN'S REQUIEM ARTIST VIEW ENT.	BUTTONERS (Knoflikari) CZECH TELEVISION
L'HOMME DE MA VIE PRESIDENT FILMS	MAX & BOBO FRANCE TELEVISION DISTRIBUTION	UNLUCKY MONKEY MOTION PICTURE PROD.ASS.OF JAPAN	CLUB VAMPIRE CONCORDE-NEW HORIZONS	GIAMAICA INTRA FILMS	RESOLUTION ALPINE PICTURES
LA RUMBERA GRUPPO MINERVA INTERNATIONAL	100 ANOS DE PERDON KEVIN WILLIAMS ASSOCIATES (KWA)	LOVE LIES BLEEDING VILLAGE ROADSHOW PICTURES	MARRIED 2 MALCOLM MARIE HOY FILMS	LE MONDE A L'ENVERS INTERMEDIA ARC PICTURES	TEAR IT DOWN ALPINE PICTURES
LUCIA PORTMAN ENTERTAINMENT	LAST LEPRECHAUN, THE PEAKVIEWING TRANSATLANTIC	UNDERCOVER ANGEL PM ENTERTAINMENT	L'ASSEDIO INTRA FILMS	ONCE WE WERE STRANGERS CURB ENTERTAINMENT	

buyers a first viewing of the film. Other key buyers may request a print to screen at their own convenience.

Ensuring that distributors know when each screening will take place is crucial. Sales agents will use the daily trade papers at the market as their main vehicle for advertising screening times, although they will also seek to alert distributors personally–through direct mailouts and telephone conversations. Because competition for the attention of buyers is very strong, many sales agents provide them with screening schedules and personal tickets.

Market screenings generally cost between $750 and $1,000. If a cinema in a city center is rented, particularly for an evening screening, the costs can rise to $2,000 to $4,000, but the film will benefit from a greater sense of exclusivity.

Press Books

Press books bring together much of the material discussed above, and will normally be produced if a film is selected for a film festival. They will be aimed at both the consumer and the trade press and designed to maximize interest in the film. A press book will usually include

• A synopsis of the film (one to two pages in length).

• Filmographies with previous credits of the producer, the director, the screenwriter, and the three or four leading cast members together with similar details on any distinguished member of the crew (e.g., a noted cinematographer or composer).

• Production notes on the film.

• A full list of cast and crew and technical information that includes running time.

In certain cases, large numbers of such press books will be required. For instance, if a film is in the official competition at the Cannes Film Festival, at least 2,000 press books, as well as at least three or four black-and-white stills from the film, are needed for those in attendance. (And the press book's text must to be in both English and French.) The total costs of such a book will be anywhere from $5,000 to $15,000. In addition, a selection of 35mm color transparencies will be supplied for magazines. The sales agent will also prepare some short clips from the film for use by television stations. These will serve as a means of boosting media coverage and raising the film's profile among the public.

Marketing Budgets During Sales

The decision about to how much money to spend on selling a film will be subject to constant modification as a picture goes through its lifestages and is presented to potential buyers. (See Lifestages chart on pages 58–59.) Much will depend on who is cash-flowing the marketing costs and who will ultimately pay those same costs–the sales agent might put up the marketing money, but normally the film's producer will eventually pay the marketing costs of selling the title. That is, the producer and sales company will agree an overall marketing budget, say between $50,000 and $300,000, to cover the life of the film. If the film is selected for a big film festival, then this is likely to be a further cost. The sales company will cover these costs, and after deducting its commission from any sales, will then recoup its marketing expenditure, with the balance being remitted to other financial backers before the balance is remitted to the producer.

Timing the Deal

A sales agent's decision about when to sell a film and a distributor's decision about when to buy a film will always depend on calculated gambles, with different factors in play each time.

For the sales agent, determining the right moment to accept an offer from a distributor will involve a strong element of risk. The sales agent may receive an offer that is below the asking price set at the first market at which the film is being sold. In the case of a film that is being pre-sold, the sales agent must decide whether to accept the offer or, in the hope of getting the asking price, wait until some the film's footage is available.

A sales agent with absolute confidence in a project may be willing to wait until it is completed. However, in other cases, a sales agent may be inclined to accept an early offer, even if it does not quite match the asking price. At this early stage, a sales agent is selling a vision of a film rather than a completed project. Once a film is screened, it will largely stand or fall on its own merits, and as a result, it will be much harder to secure a good price for relatively indifferent material.

Similarly, a distributor must decide when is the best time to make an offer for a film. A bid on a film that is felt to be particularly strong may better be made at the pre-sale stage rather than after the picture is completed, when prices may rise. Conversely, for some films, particularly those in the $8- to $15-million budget range, sellers will ask for a relatively high minimum guarantee, yet the buyer may feel that the ingredients of the package (stars, director, and script), as laid out on paper, do not immediately justify the asking price. As a result, the distributor will insist on waiting to view the finished film.

Because some territories (Scandinavia, for example) have a relatively limited number of distributors, there is less competition for pictures. As a result, distributors in these territories can afford to be very selective in their approach to buying pictures–often, they will wait to see a finished film before deciding whether to acquire it. Buyers in other territories (for example, Korea) tend to have very specific ideas about the kinds of pictures they want–they will be prepared to wait to view a completed film to see if it meets their specified criteria, which will vary from year to year, according to changes in the market.

■ Festivals

The principle aims of screening a film at a festival are to reach those potential buyers who, for whatever reason, did not buy the film at an earlier stage and to stir up interest in the film among the press and sometimes even the public.

The marketing materials that will accompany a festival screening are, in essence, the same as those used for a screening at a market, although the target festival audience will be somewhat wider, since in many cases, the public will also be attending.

A festival screening will often mark the first time that critics have had a chance to review a picture. The reviews from those critics will be particularly important in determining

> *" The marketing materials that will accompany a festival screening are, in essence, the same as those used for a screening at a market. "*

the likely box-office success of arthouse films. Such a film's poor review from an influential critic in a particular country will invariably hurt the box office, while a good review can substantially enhance the salability a film that otherwise appears to have very few tangible marketing hooks.

The fact that members of the public are allowed to attend most of the annual film festivals around the world means that a festival screening will often be the first time that a picture is seen by a general audience. The public's reaction to this screening will have an impact on a film's subsequent performance: If an audience likes a film, it will be likely to recommend that film to friends and colleagues, generating favorable word of mouth prior to the film's release and boosting the film's chances of success. Conversely, a poor reception by a festival audience will invariably hinder a film's subsequent box-office performance.

The most important film festival is the Festival International du Film, also known as the Cannes International Film Festival. Screenings at Cannes are restricted to those with special passes or invitations and, as with most film festivals, are divided into a number of different sections.

Before entering a film for consideration for a festival screening at Cannes, the sales agent or distributor will need to have a high level of confidence in it, since a bad reception at Cannes can paralyze a film's chances of success. In many cases, a film will be reviewed by many of the most influential critics from high-profile consumer and trade publications around the world, so bad reviews can fast become universal. A film must also be strong enough to stand out from its competition, because many hundreds of films will be screened during the festival and market.

The distributor or sales agent must decide which section of Cannes will be most appropriate for a given title. The most prestigious section of the festival is the Official Selection, which includes films being shown in competition for the Palme d'Or prize, a handful of titles shown out of competition, and some twenty-five smaller, more intimate films in the section Un Certain Regard. Winners of the Palme d'Or over the last decade have included *Secrets and Lies, Pulp Fiction, The Piano, The Best Intentions, Underground, Barton Fink, Wild at Heart,* and *sex, lies and videotape.*

The films chosen for the official competition will have the highest profile during the festival, since they will each receive a gala screening that will invariably be attended by leading figures from all sections of the film industry (from actors to potential distributors) and journalists. The official competition will usually consist of a mix of titles that ranges from mainstream, commercial pictures to more specialized, arthouse films.

The other important section at Cannes is la Quinzaine des Réalisateurs (Directors' Fortnight), which tends to screen smaller, more intimate films than those in the Official Selection. Entering a film in this section may ensure that it has a better chance to shine, rather than competing with the high-profile titles that dominate the official competition.

A third section of note, La Semaine de la Critique (Critics' Week), which screens seven films, can also give a film a unique profile. Films properly positioned within the above two events have a chance to create an international impact. *Muriel's Wedding* and Stephen Frears' *The Snapper* were launched in the Directors' Fortnight, while 1997 Academy Award winner for Best Foreign Film, *Karacter* by Dutch director Mike van Diem, was in Critics' Week.

Entering Cannes is a competition in itself—over 600 films are seen by Festival director Gilles Jacob and his team before they decide on the forty or fifty films that will be screened in the Official Selection, while the heads of the other two sections seek films from around the world in order to present their best line-up.

If a film receives a positive response at a Cannes screening, favorable reports will travel very rapidly around the festival by word of mouth. As a result, potential buyers will soon be heading to the office of the film's sales agent, so the sales agent will need to ensure that all marketing materials have been carefully prepared in advance.

Competing at Cannes is a costly business. The costs are likely to be at least $50,000, and can often go far higher, depending on how elaborate a party one throws and how much is spent to bring and accommodate talent for the festival.

The other key festivals include Sundance in January, Berlin in February and Venice in September. Like Cannes, these festivals will generally only consider films that have not yet screened at other festivals and that have been released in few, if any, territories. Many hundreds of other film festivals (of varying importance) are held around the world. New York, Telluride, and Toronto are particularly strong festivals. In some cases, a sales agent may choose to enter a film in a lesser-known festival where it will have a greater chance of standing out, rather than in an event where it might be swamped by a deluge of high-profile films.

Often, a film's sales agent will work in close conjunction with that film's local distributor when trying to get the film selected for a particular festival. A festival screening will offer an important opportunity to raise a title's profile in a local distributor's own territory.

In the case of the most prestigious festivals, the sales agent will usually attend the event. For other festivals, where the film has primarily been entered to boost awareness in the particular territory where the festival is held, the sales agent will not attend, since it will often be the local distributor who will have chosen to enter the film in that particular event.

This section has examined the importance of markets and festivals as a means of selling a film to distributors, securing press coverage, and making initial contact with a target audience. Once a film has been sold, its distributor will start to implement a marketing strategy that may build on some of the elements employed by the sales agent, but which will be much wider in scope. In the following section, we will examine the tools that a distributor uses to maximize a marketing strategy's effectiveness in the run-up to a film's release.

Film Distribution in Europe

For each individual film, a distributor must arrive at a marketing strategy that promises the best possible chance of maximizing the film's audience.

As emphasized earlier in this book, distributors must have a means of attracting the consumer to their particular films in the face of competition from other films, other leisure activities, and such other forms of audiovisual entertainment as video and television, which, in many cases, may be cheaper and more convenient for the consumer. Film distribution is a business that seeks to maximize its share of a limited pot of consumer expenditure and leisure time.

This section will address the strategies used by distributors to motivate the general public to pay to see a film on the big screen. But before doing so, it will examine the environment in which distributors in various European countries operate.

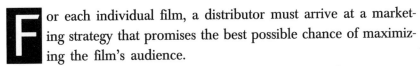Key Concepts in Film Distribution

Since every film involves a unique combination of elements, the marketing of individual pictures, unlike the marketing of many other goods, cannot rely simply on consumer preference for certain tried and tested ingredients. However, an audience may desire to see a film because of its stars, content, or director. Sequels to successful films offer a similar opportunity to build on an audience's taste. But the value of such "brand names" in selling a film is never assured because many other elements (personal recommendations, reviews, and so on) influence audience demand for a specific picture.

The films and filmmakers that have managed to create brand-name value are relatively few in number. In many cases, Walt Disney (the Hollywood studio) is able to use the perceived value of the Disney brand name to help sell its films because it has a reputation for producing high-quality, entertaining films, particularly animated features, for children. The films from the pairing of producer Ismail Merchant and director James Ivory, who specialize in period literary adaptations featuring quality production values, are another example of identifiable branding. The term "Merchant-Ivory production" connotes a specific type of film (*A Room With a View, Howard's End, The Remains of the Day*) that is likely to have a clearly defined target audience. Such directors as Martin Scorsese, Francis Coppola, Oliver Stone, and Quentin Tarantino, because of their particular cinematic styles, have also become "brand names."

Preview screenings for targeted audiences can be invaluable way to spread awareness of a film and build its want-to-see factor among the public. For example, 20th Century Fox, the U.K. distributor of *The Full Monty*, gave away 100,000 tickets for a series of special previews. The film subsequently grossed over $87 million in the U.K., becoming the second biggest 1997 U.K. box-office earner after *Titanic* ($108 million). Similarly, prior to its U.K. release of *Sliding Doors* (starring Gwyneth Paltrow), UIP gave away 40,000 to 50,000 tickets. *Sliding Doors* went on to gross $20 million in the U.K., becoming the seventh most popular film released there in 1998.

A distributor's primary task is to define a film's target audience, and then to create and sustain that audience's awareness of the film—the target audience must know that the film is being released and have some idea of its most appealing elements. This awareness must then be translated into want-to-see, so that the audience has a desire to pay to view it on the big screen.

> **"** Awareness of a film does not simply materialize from thin air. It has to be created. **"**

Awareness of a film does not simply materialize from thin air. It has to be created through a process that involves advertising, word-of-mouth (the personal recommendations of those who have already seen the film), reviews, and many other elements. Want-to-see is difficult to create because an audience's desire to see a film will depend heavily on their subjective judgment of it.

Word-of-mouth is a very powerful (if not the most powerful) determinant of a film's theatrical life. Even if a film opens well, poor or negative word-of-mouth is likely to kill its possible long-term box-office success.

The key for the distributor seeking to build word-of-mouth is to determine, before a film's release, the kind of people who will be most influential in spreading good or bad opinions. These opinion makers can be people working within the industry (distributors, exhibitors, designers, etc.), who represent the film's first audience; the media, which has an influence over the general public; and specific consumer target groups (see section on Market Research).

Once a film has opened, its distributor can tell very quickly from the box-office results if it has been successfully positioned to reach the avid cinemagoers and convert their awareness of it into want-to-see. During a film's second week of release, the percentage drop in admissions will be a crucial indicator of its likely playing time–the steeper the drop, the shorter the period for which the exhibitor is likely to want to play the film. Occasionally, a film's takings may increase after its opening release, which was the case for the U.K. release of *The Full Monty*, but this is very much the exception to the rule.

Few films grow popular with time, particularly arthouse films because exhibitors or bookers rarely have the confidence to let such films build an audience in this way. It is therefore essential that as many opinion-formers as possible should be attracted to the cinema during a film's the opening week (or weekend), so that they can recommend the film to their peers. From this base, a film's eventual run will be determined.

"Few films grow popular with time."

The distributor will set out to maximize awareness, want-to-see, and word-of-mouth by creating a marketing plan that is designed to enable a film to reach its audience. This process is known as "positioning" a film.

Just as a sales agent must find the best way of positioning a film for the international buyers in the industry, so a distributor must find the best way of positioning a film for its potential audience.

The nature of a particular film will be an important factor in its positioning. The process of positioning a mainstream thriller, which is likely to appeal to a broad audience, is very different from the process used for an intimate drama from an arthouse director. While, in most cases, a mainstream picture's marketing budget will be very much higher than an arthouse film's marketing budget, this is by no means the sole distinction between selling the two titles to the cinemagoer.

The focus of a mainstream film's marketing campaign will often be the film's stars, who will usually be featured prominently on its poster. Posters of this sort, designed to entice a broad audience, will often employ large head-shots of the key players set against a backdrop shot from the film. Examples of this style are found in the poster art for *Face Off,* with Nicholas Cage and John Travolta; *Saving Private Ryan,* with Tom Hanks; and *As Good as It Gets,* with Jack Nicholson.

The poster for an arthouse film that has less recognizable stars attached will often feature the director's name if that director's previous films have been successful. For example, posters for films by Ang Lee, Hal Hartley, David Lynch, and Woody Allen will play up the popularity of these directors' names. Without known stars or a known director, posters will often play up the film's genre.

Marketing hooks can also vary. For example, specialized films that have enjoyed great crossover success, such as *The English Patient* and *Shakespeare In Love,* have often used their initial critical acclaim as a hook to attract a wider audience. Such films are platformed in key cities where they are likely to generate strong critical responses that will influence the rest of the market. Their rollout pattern of releasing prints to key cities will take place over a period of three to five weeks, allowing sufficient time for word-of-mouth to spread. More mainstream films, which generally have higher marketing budgets, will go out with a large number of prints and often employ television advertising, which smaller, independent films may not be able to afford.

> *" The effort and skill required to position a small film effectively can be considerably greater than that required for a much larger film. "*

The effort and skill required to position a small film effectively can be considerably greater than that required for a much larger film. Positioning a small film involves targeting specialized audiences, which may be difficult through conventional channels. Identifying those elements of a film that are likely to appeal to such audiences may also be difficult.

■ The Structure of Film Distribution in Europe

In 1996, the distribution arms of the U.S. majors accounted, on average, for 63.2% of box-office revenues in each local European market, which was down from 72.5% of box-office revenues in 1991, reflecting the increasing popularity of national films in many countries. Each U.S. major tends to release between twenty and thirty pictures a year, most of which are produced by their own production arms, however some of which will be negative pickups–films that have been acquired from independent producers once they have completed principal photography or at some stage during postproduction.

While such U.S. studios as Columbia Tri-Star, 20th Century Fox, and Warner Bros. usually use their own distribution arms to handle their pictures internationally, other studios have formed joint ventures to distribute their films overseas. Outside the U.S., most films from Paramount, Universal, and MGM are released through United International Pictures (UIP), while the overseas distribution arm of Disney, in most European territories, is Buena Vista International. In France, Disney has created a joint-venture partnership with Gaumont, an independent distributor, while Fox and UGC have created a distribution venture in France called UFD and New Line has formed a long-term alliance with five European distributors.

A number of European distribution companies have also begun operating on a pan-European basis. The French group Pathé has distribution operations or alliances in France (AMLF), Germany (Tobis), and the U.K. (Pathé). Prior to its sale to Universal, PolyGram had created a London-based global film distribution arm that had operations in a dozen territories, including the U.K., France, Germany, Spain, Italy, and the U.S.

Creating distribution subsidiaries of any reasonable size in a variety of countries is capital intensive (the bulk of this capital is required to support the costs of prints and advertising). At present, each distribution subsidiary releases films independently because market conditions and the structure of the media differ so widely from country to country that little would be achieved from simultaneous releases.

Most of the other films released in Europe that are not handled by the companies discussed above are handled by a few large local distribution companies that release between ten and thirty titles per year. Such major national independents as AMLF, Bac Films in France, Cecchi Gori in Italy, Pathé in the U.K., Lauren Films in Spain, and Neue Constantin in Germany usually have formal output deals (or at least a loose informal alliance) with at least one indigenous production company and several international sales companies.

An output deal is an agreement struck between a distribution company and an international sales company or a producer that gives a distributor rights to a number of pictures over a period of time. This type of agreement makes the task of a sales company or a producer easier because they no longer have to be concerned about finding a distributors for their agreement-specified pictures in specific territories. From a distributor's viewpoint, an output deal gives guaranteed access to a slate of films against which they can amortize their overheads. Distributors who do not have the benefit of output deals with specific companies must constantly worry about acquiring enough pictures to distribute and make a return on their investments.

Film distribution is a high-risk business—only a handful of titles will enjoy substantial profits, while most pictures lose money on their theatrical run. An industry rule of thumb is that seven out of ten pictures will lose money on their theatrical release, two will break-even, and one will do extremely well. Therefore, distributors try to ensure that they have a sufficiently broad spread of films, so that the profits from a handful of successful pictures will outweigh the losses incurred by their other films.

The remainder of the market–that which is not controlled by the U.S. ma-

jors and the large local distributors–is controlled by distributors that specialize in arthouse films or re-releases. Many small, niche distributors that handle just two or three films a year exist in France and Germany. In the U.K., a considerable number of these independent distributors have hit financial difficulty, although a few major independents, such as Entertainment and Pathé, are able to spend relatively high sums on prints and advertising (P&A).

For independent distributors, a sound understanding of the competitive advantages enjoyed by the U.S. majors is important because it will help them design marketing and distribution strategies that offer an effective alternative to the major Hollywood studios. What are the structural factors that enable the U.S. distributors to maintain their market position, and what impact do these factors have on the independent distributor?

■ Economies of Scale

As explained in Section 3, the Hollywood studios have a vertically-integrated structure that spans development, production, distribution, and, in some cases, exhibition and guarantees them a constant flow of major pictures. This continuous volume of films enables them to spread their risks across many pictures, so that the rewards from a few highly profitable ones will easily outweigh the losses from others. The U.S. studios also have large capital bases that are underwritten by their vast, well-exploited libraries.

The U.S. studios are able to guarantee a certain volume of high-profile pictures each year, which gives them great leverage in negotiating such terms as release dates (playdates) with the cinema chains. The ability to control a film's release date can be crucial because certain weeks of the year, particularly holiday periods, may be especially favorable for releasing a film while other time slots may be much weaker. It all depends on the type of picture country in which it is being released.

The rapidly rising costs of release–prints and advertising materials–have hit the independents hard. The rate-card prices of prints and advertising are the same for both the independents and the U.S. majors, but the majors will often buy in bulk for a guaranteed supply of films, giving them considerable negotiating strength with suppliers in this sphere. The Hollywood majors also have the advantage of being able to partly subsidize their P&A costs with the significant revenues they accrue from the sale of pay-TV rights in the U.K., France, and elsewhere.

By contrast, most independent distributors in Europe, even allowing for any output deals they might have, cannot guarantee their exhibitors and other end-users a steady stream of films over a long period of time. These distributors are also usually dependent on acquiring their films from independent third parties and, therefore, often unable to rely on receiving their films at a given time because independent distributors in Europe have much less leverage than the majors when it comes to exerting pressure on producers to meet a target release date.

In addition to their vertical integration, the U.S. majors also benefit from horizontal integration–they operate large distribution structures on an international scale with offices in virtually every territory they serve around the world. This enables them to coordinate their marketing across a large number of countries and enjoy "economies of scale" in such areas as market research and star junkets. For example, the majors will heavily test their films and trailers and posters, and then send this research information along to all of the territories where they will be releasing their films. The majors also use their long-standing relationships with acting talent to persuade their actors to do international press tours, which is something that few independent distributors can arrange with any consistency. Additionally, the majors have large in-house marketing departments that few independents can rival. Through their in-house marketing departments, the majors can get a jump on creating advance awareness of their films by delivering key marketing materials (trailers, posters, standees, etc.) to their foreign distribution outlets much earlier than most independents can.

In Europe, screens are scattered across thirty different countries, which often means that different campaigns must be created for different audiences with different languages. Because of their coordinated network of international offices, the U.S. studios are able to centralize the release of their films across several territories. One result of this setup is that the majors can enjoy the impact of a single poster image that is seen across several territories. U.S. studios are also easily able to exploit a film's success in the U.S. as a means of generating extra publicity. For example, *Four Weddings and a Funeral*, a British film, opened in the United States before it opened in the U.K., where it was subsequently advertised as "America's No. 1 Smash-Hit Comedy."

For the independent distributor, any delay in obtaining prints and marketing tools can significantly hurt a film's performance. To maximize the chances of success at the box office, the producer and the sales agent must deliver all materials to the distributor on time. Independent European distributors usually have one or two people responsible for chasing down marketing tools (photos, posters, brochures, advertising campaign material, etc.), and most have expressed dissatisfaction over the fact that such materials nearly always arrive late. Good servicing is a key element in the positioning of a film in its various markets. It should not be neglected.

> *"To maximize the chances of success at the box office, the producer and the sales agent must deliver all materials to the distributor on time."*

Concentration on a Few Star-Driven Titles

The bulk of the annual box-office revenues in each European territory comes from twenty or so films that attract some fifty percent of the total admissions. Many of these pictures are star-driven films distributed by the major U.S. studios, although smaller arthouse pictures distributed by independent European distributors are finding an increasing audience.

The dominance of the U.S. majors is based not on the volume of pictures they release—in many cases, the combined number of pictures released by local distributors is considerably greater than that handled by the studios. Instead, the strength the U.S. majors' distribution operations is based on the high level of success achieved by a relatively small number of titles, while the smaller revenues achieved by independents are generated by a larger number of films.

As stated earlier, the U.S. majors may release between twenty and thirty pictures in a given year, but just a few—such sufficiently large box-office winners as *Jurassic Park*, *Titanic*, and *Men in Black*—will result in handsome profits. Film distribution is like roulette—success is not guaranteed, but the profits from one win can easily outstrip the costs of a string of losses.[1] Generally, independent distributors, with some notable exceptions, do not have access to such high-earning, star-driven films, although they may well have pictures that are capable of more limited commercial success in the marketplace.

In many cases, the independents will use the marketing exposure they gain from a film's theatrical release as a loss-leader, offsetting these losses against the money they will make from the film's video and television release. Therefore, the fall-off in the growth of the video market has greatly affected the independents. When video

---

[1] One guide to a film's success is the measure of its revenues as a multiple of its budget—the higher the ratio, the more successful the film.

rental was stronger, many European independents were able to survive on so-called B-movies, which did not feature well-known stars or name directors, yet had clearly identifiable genres, usually action-adventure. But at the end of the 1980s, the video rental market began to change, and the kinds of titles that succeeded on video became much closer to those that did well in the cinema–high-quality films featuring known stars and directors. As a result, in many instances, independents were no longer able to rely on video as a means of offsetting losses incurred on theatrical distribution. Although the emergence of pay-TV in the late 1980s provided some compensation for the decline in video rental, the films that succeed with pay-TV audiences also tend to be star-driven.

It should not be assumed that, simply because the major U.S. studios have the aforementioned strategic advantages, the position of the independent European distributor is hopeless. Rather, for all the reasons cited above, the independent distributors' strategies deployed for maximizing the effectiveness of their films must be very different from those used by the studios.

The U.S. majors will frequently use costly advertising campaigns across a variety of media (newspapers, magazines, television, radio, billboards, and any other available means) to ensure that international audiences are aware of their films. The cost of such large-scale campaigns keep them well beyond the financial means of most independent European distributors, but the independents' efficient and creative use of resources is a critical weapon that can be used to compensate for limited budgets. The sheer volume of money thrown at a marketing campaign is, after all, not necessarily an index of its effectiveness. The use of subtlety and humor, combined with a close understanding of local audiences, can often be considerably more cost-effective than an expensive hard-sell approach.

As we have stressed throughout this book, every film is unique and requires specific marketing strategies to create awareness and want-to-see, and the methods that are used to achieve this can be clearly identified. To determine a particular approach for a specific film, a distributor planning a release campaign will set out to answer a number of questions, which will usually include the following:

• How should the film be positioned?

• What elements of the film have strong marketing potential?

• Who is the picture's target audience, and does the picture have the ability to cross over to other audiences?

• When is the optimum time for releasing the film?

• How much should be spent on prints and advertising?

• How is the film best promoted in terms of paid advertising, publicity, and promotion?

The following material address each of these questions in turn.

The film distributor in each territory, often working in conjunction with the film's producer (and in some territories, its director), has the task of positioning the film in a way that will maximize its level of awareness and want-to-see among its target audience. How do distributors set about doing this?

Distributors must first determine the type of film that they are selling to the public. This determination is critical to the picture's positioning because it helps to define the target audience and influences the entire style of the marketing campaign. For example, the poster, the trailer, and the promotional tie-ins used for a mainstream horror film will emphasize very different elements from those used for an intimate arthouse drama. Sometimes, a film may combine elements of several genres, for instance, a thriller with a strong love interest. Such a cross-genre picture allows the distributor to simultaneously position it for two distinct types of audience. In other cases, the director's name may signify that the film is clearly an arthouse film—one that will appeal to a specialized audience that is primarily composed of relatively affluent, educated people living in urban areas.

" Unconvincing positioning of a film will have a negative effect on the consumer's perception of that film, and may hurt its box-office performance. "

Defining its genre—even multiple genres—is the first step to positioning a film. Often, determining the nature of a film is relatively easy, based on the ingredients of its story that may refer to the conventions of a specific genre. Once the film has been identified as belonging to a specific category (e.g., romantic comedy), that category will usually determine the best way to position it for audiences throughout Europe. If, however, the audience has difficulty identifying the genre of the film, that may indicate that the distributor is uncertain about the type of picture it is selling. Unconvincing positioning of a film will have a negative effect on the consumer's perception of that film, and may hurt its box-office performance.

While the specific nature of a marketing campaign may differ from country to country, a film's generic positioning will be broadly similar from country to country because its generic elements will tend to appeal to similar target groups in most European territories. Since, for the reasons already stated, the release of a given film across the various European territories is usually staggered, this similarity in the way it is positioned enables the distribution arms of the Hollywood studios to learn from the reaction to the film in one territory as they prepare the film for release elsewhere.

By contrast, it may be harder for independent distributors to determine how to position a film for a particular country, because some of the films they handle may be perceived as mainstream pictures in one territory and as arthouse pictures in another. Therefore, independent distributors must take particular care to ensure that a film's appropriate target audience has been identified. Distributors should not simply assume that the way in which a film was positioned in one country will be appropriate for another territory, where the film may carry a very different appeal.

■ Positioning Pictures That Don't Fit Traditional Categories

Distributors of all kinds, especially independent distributors, will often find themselves handling films that do not fit neatly into either arthouse or commercial categories. For instance, some arthouse or specialized pictures have the potential to reach more commercial audiences. Examples of such pictures are *Boogie Nights, Fargo, The English Patient,* and *Elizabeth.* Similarly, some commercial films, often those falling into the $5- to $15-million budget range and featuring known stars and a known director, once completed, may not turn out to be sufficiently commercial for a wide release, yet may not be specialized enough for release in arthouse cinemas. The distributor will often have bought such a film at the script stage or while it was in preproduction, anticipating that it would be suitable for a wide theatrical release. On paper, such a film's ingredients—its story, its stars, and its director's track record—may indicate that it has commercial potential. But on viewing the completed film, the distributor may realize that money spent on a wide theatrical release is unlikely to be recouped at the box office. However, the distributor may still launch a small theatrical release to create the vital exposure that can help maximize a film's video potential and eventually enable it to recoup its costs.

In some cases, a distributor will be contractually obliged to release a film theatrically, prior to its appearance on video, simply to secure this type of exposure. In such cases, the distributor will need to create a cost-effective campaign built on certain core elements, such as the appeal of the film's stars, while also ensuring that other elements of the film, such as a particularly unusual storyline, are used to try to broaden the film's audience. The aim of this campaign is not only to reach the general public but also to influence the video distributors and to help promote the title when it is eventually shipped out to video rental shops.

Many of a film's elements can be used to make it attractive to the public. The distributor must identify these elements and translate them into an effective marketing campaign. The ability to find and then exploit these elements is a skill that can often go a long way toward overcoming the constraints of a limited marketing budget. Five key elements that can be used to help sell a picture have been singled out below.

■ Exploiting a Film's Assets

A film's stars and its director are a crucial selling points for many mainstream commercial films, as well as for some arthouse films. Their names will frequently help secure publicity for a film, which may be particularly useful in the case of films that do not have large prints and advertising budgets and are dependent on reviews and press coverage. Securing press coverage will always be easier if a film's stars and/or its director are well known because their names will help newspaper and magazine publishers maximize their sales and help television programs boost their ratings.

Stars

The mere presence of a star is no guarantee of box-office success, but a star's name will often be the central plank of a publicity and advertising campaign because it will give a distributor its best chance of maximizing awareness of a film among its target audience. If a film's stars are judged to be of value in selling a film, they will be featured heavily in its poster campaign, its trailer, and any radio or television advertising.

> *" The mere presence of a star is no guarantee of box-office success. "*

A distributor will also try to persuade a film's stars to tour individual territories to promote the film and to give interviews to the media so that the film secures widespread editorial coverage.[2] If a star will not tour, a distributor may attempt to arrange telephone interviews or to fly that star to a prominent festival and arrange for interviews there with both the local and the foreign press. The popular

---

[2] The ways in which such goals can be achieved is discussed in The Essential Ingredients of an Advertising Campaign.

press will frequently be targeted when trying to secure interviews with stars because most films that feature well-known stars will be aimed at readers of these types of publications.

While such American stars as Leonard Di Caprio, Tom Cruise, and Bruce Willis have massive box-office appeal, on a more limited scale, some European stars, such as Juliette Binoche, Victoria Abril, Emma Thompson and Daniel Day-Lewis, have the ability to attract fairly broad international audiences. However, other than a small handful of names, the value of European stars will usually be confined to their home territories.[3] (It has been argued in some quarters that the absence of European stars is a drawback for European films because it deprives them of a marketing hook.)

The Director

In Europe, a director's name can be particularly important in helping to create audience awareness and want-to-see. This reflects the influence of the auteur theory, which originally emerged in France during the 1950s, and, in its more extreme manifestations, saw the director as the sole guiding vision behind a film. Usually, a director's name is most important when marketing an arthouse film to relatively well-educated, urban audiences. Exploiting a well-known director's name gives a certain brand-name value to a film in the eyes of its potential audience. It tells filmgoers that, based on their knowledge of previous work by that director, they are about to watch a certain kind of film. The announcement of a new film by a well-known director is often enough in itself to trigger the curiosity and anticipation of avid cinemagoers and film critics who will start talking about the film before they have even seen it.

A director's name may feature prominently in a film's poster campaign and its trailer. As with well-known stars, a distributor may try to persuade a director to tour individual territories to promote a film

---

[3]Most actors who have box-office value across a number of European countries usually have received a very significant boost from exposure in successful Hollywood films.

and give interviews to the media, although the target media for such coverage–usually, the arts sections of serious newspapers and heavy-weight magazines–may be quite different from that employed for star interviews.

Even if the names of the stars and directors are not enough in themselves to create a high level of want-to-see, they can often be extremely useful in raising the awareness of a film among its primary targeted audience and the critics who influence the core audience. Since awareness is the first step toward want-to-see, the name of a star or a director with some notoriety can prove to be the first hook on which a distributor can build a marketing campaign.

Regardless of the name value of a film's director and its stars, the largest factor in determining the eventual success or failure of a film will usually be its combination of strong performances, script, and production values.

Exploiting a Film's Genre and Story Ingredients

A distributor attempts to use a film's genre (e.g., action thriller, romantic comedy, period drama) as a marketing hook. The aim here is not to give the story away but to inform the audience about the kind of film that they can expect, for example, a comedy rather than a psychological drama.

The design of a film's poster and trailer should clearly reflect its genre if this is felt to be a particularly strong selling point. By using particular images from a film, a distributor will be able to signal to the target audience that a picture belongs to a genre with which they are familiar, and which they may be expected to enjoy. Not only the visual image on the poster but also the quotes used from reviewers can help reinforce the impression that a film belongs to a particular genre.

Most Hollywood films operate within specific genre categories that can be identified with relative ease. One type of film that can easily be identified in generic terms is the comedy. Although comedies perform very strongly at the box office within their country of origin, they achieve limited impact abroad.

Sequels to a successful film, which exploit a tested formula, are a well-established and often highly profitable segment of the film industry. For the distributor, the mere fact that a film is a sequel to a successful original is a strong selling point. The marketing campaign for a sequel will be able to exploit the similarity between the two pictures, persuading the audience that they will have a chance once more to enjoy many of the elements that drew them to the original film, but in the context of a fresh story.

When marketing a sequel, a distributor will also have a rather clear idea of its core audience, based on the original film's audience. This will make it easier to position such a film in terms of its marketing concept and the selection the advertising media that will be most effective in reaching its target audience. In some cases, however, a distributor will also try to attract those people who did not see the original film, and so will look for new marketing hooks that might help capture this audience.

Using Awards

As was discussed in the Markets and Festivals section of this book, festival awards can be extremely useful tools when designing campaigns for certain types of films, particularly arthouse pictures. An award from a festival is often a sign that a film represents a particularly fine example of its genre, especially if the award is from a festival devoted to a specific film genre.[4] The seal of approval by a prestigious international jury will provide a tangible hook for the distributor to use when building an advertising and publicity campaign.

If a distributor makes effective use of such marketing hooks, media interest in a film will increase, which will, in turn, serve substantially to raise awareness of the title among its target audience. A distributor may mention a film's award on its poster, in its trailer, or in other

---

[4] One such festival that is devoted to a specific film genre is the festival of Vevey (held in August in Switzerland), which concentrates on comedy films.

advertising materials. In some cases, the distinctive logo of a festival award may be incorporated into a film's poster artwork.

The most important awards for independent films, in terms of the free publicity they generate, are the top prizes from such international film festivals as Cannes (including the Camera d'Or for best first film), Sundance, Venice, and Berlin. A host of specialized festivals are also held in America and around the world (details of these ever-changing events are available in the film trade publications). However, the impact of such awards on cinema admissions is always difficult to predict because any given film's box-office performance may be affected by many other variables.[5]

In the case of mainstream films, the Oscars, which are awarded by the Academy of Motion Picture Arts and Sciences (AMPAS) in the last week of March, can have an enormous impact on the performance of a film, both in terms of its theatrical release and its video release, because the media from around the world extensively cover

> " A picture may often benefit simply from being nominated for an award, since a nomination does a great deal to raise the public profile of a film. "

Oscar nominees and, especially, winners.[6] The Golden Globes, awarded in January by the Hollywood Foreign Press Association, may also raise a picture's public profile.

A picture may often benefit simply from being nominated for an award, since a nomination does a great deal to raise the public profile of a film. Foreign distributors will often plan the release of films that may be potential nominees for an award to coincide with the unveiling of the nominations, and so benefit from the attendant publicity.

---

[5] See the section on the Cannes Film Festival pp. 54–55.

[6] "Conventional wisdom is that an Oscar is worth an additional $20 to $35 million at the box office. Another much-vaunted industry tenet contends that a Best Picture Oscar boosts revenues by some fifteen percent worldwide." *Variety*, February 22, 1993.

Exploiting Performances in Other Territories

A film's previous success in a foreign territory is a marketing hook that can be used by a distributor who's preparing the release of that film in his home country, because such previous success will often raise the local media's awareness of a film. However, the territory where the film succeeded has to be among the key cinema markets and the film's success has to be extraordinary, commercially and/or critically. For example, the Italian box-office performance of Roberto Benigni's *Life is Beautiful* (which was sold internationally by Miramax) and its Grand Jury Prize at the 1998 Cannes Film festival were often cited by the foreign media as the film started to open around the world after its Italian release.

Wherever appropriate, a distributor will play up a film's foreign successes when approaching the local media to try to secure editorial coverage. Although a distributor has little, if any, influence over foreign coverage, such exposure will be enormously helpful because national journalists are likely to be aware of a particular picture because of its foreign successes.

In certain cases, a national distributor may wish to incorporate quotes from foreign media into a film's publicity material. This is often the case in the U.K., where certain U.S. publications–which include *Time* Magazine, the *New York Times*, and the *Los Angeles Times*–carry quite a bit of weight. The fact that many foreign publications devote considerable space to Hollywood films and their stars, not to mention the worldwide impact of today's Internet and the worldwide broadcasting outlets (e.g., CNN), means that certain U.S. films will attract considerable international attention through coverage in their own U.S. publications.

Generally speaking, a strong performance by a U.S. film at the U.S. box office will also be a valuable element for many European distributors as they plan their marketing campaign for that film.

■ Who Is the Target Audience for a Film?

Before a distributor starts to plan and implement a film's marketing campaign, identifying that film's target audience is vital. When defining a target audience, the factors that will be taken into account are age, gender, social class, and income level. As a distributor determines which segments of the population he will try to reach with a given film, these categories will help him pinpoint that audience.

In terms of age, Europe has four main groups of cinemagoers:

• Children aged 7 through 14 years
• Young adults aged 15 through 24 years
• Adults aged 25 through 34 years
• Adults over age 35

The core group of cinemagoers in Europe are young adults between the ages of 15 and 24. Many members of this demographic group go to the cinema at least once a month. They also tend to be highly responsive to trends, and film marketing campaigns can often exploit their desire to identify with certain fashions. In many countries, the adult audience goes to the cinema, on average, less than once a year.

A distributor will also set out to identify a film's target audience on the basis of a film's ingredients, such as subject matter, genre, and featured stars. Certain genres, such as romance, will tend to appeal more to women, while action-adventure is a more male-oriented genre. And certain stars will have a predominantly male following, while others will appeal primarily to females.

A distributor's knowledge of which elements are likely to appeal to which segments of the population will be guided in part by the past track record of films in a similar genre or which featured particular stars. But, as has been repeatedly emphasized, because each film is a unique entity, it will never be sufficient to assume that, for example, just because a certain film featuring a certain star appealed strongly to women between the ages of 15 and 20, that the same will apply to the next feature in which that star appears.

104

MARKETING AND
SELLING
YOUR FILM
AROUND THE
WORLD

A distributor will also seek to determine whether a film's appeal might be widened beyond its immediate target audience. In many cases, a distributor will seek to identify a film's primary audience together with a secondary audience.

■ Determining the Date and Pattern of a Film's Release

After a distributor has identified a film's target audience and set a P&A budget, three key questions must be asked:
- When should the film be released?
- With what number of prints should it be released?
- In which cinemas should it be released?

The answers to these questions will be heavily influenced by what other films are playing in the marketplace at the time.

Before examining the optimum release dates and the typical release patterns in Europe, we need to explore the relationship between the distributor and the exhibitor.

■ The Relationship Between Distributor and Exhibitor

To reach the paying public, a distributor must first license a film to an exhibitor. The relationship between distributor and exhibitor is essentially that of supplier to retailer. But with power increasingly concentrated in the cinema chains, the negotiating muscle of independent distributors has eroded in some European territories (especially in France and Italy).

In most instances a distributor will show a film to an exhibitor prior to that exhibitor's decision to license it. However, in some instances, an exhibitor may have to license a film without seeing it. This is particularly the case with large U.S. films, which are booked into cinema circuits well ahead of release. If an exhibitor likes a film, a decision will be jointly made with the distributor as to when the film will open, how many prints will go out, and how the release will subsequently develop.

The exhibitor and the distributor will also jointly determine the percentage deal, which will indicate the split of gross receipts between the distributor and the exhibitor and other parties and, in some cases, the length of the run. The percentage that the exhibitor pays to the distributor, which is known as the "net rental" or the "distributor's gross receipts," is negotiable and varies from country to country. It ranges from a low of twenty-five percent of the box-office to a high of seventy percent, with a typical fifty-fifty split on the first net rentals.[7]

> *"Targeting the right cinema for a particular film is an important part of a distributor's marketing strategy."*

A distributor deals with many types of exhibitors, ranging from large cinema chains that control hundreds of screens to small independent operators who own only one cinema. Depending on the nature of the particular film they are handling, distributors will approach the specific types of exhibitors that they feel are be best suited to the title. Targeting the right cinema for a particular film is an important part of a distributor's marketing strategy. To do this, the distributor has to know the seating capacity of the cinema and the type of audience that it usually attracts. Identifying a cinema's audience profile is particularly important for specialized films that target niche audiences.

Mainstream pictures will predominantly be booked into the major cinema chains, while arthouse pictures will tend to be targeted at the

---

[7] See Section 6.

106

MARKETING AND
SELLING
YOUR FILM
AROUND THE
WORLD

independent houses. For films that are felt to have crossover potential, both types of cinemas may be used, as well as upmarket urban cinemas.

Certain cinemas will create an identity that inexorably associates them with arthouse films. This will be done not only through their programming strategy but also by installing such facilities as coffee bars or bookshops, which are likely to appeal to an arthouse audience. Moreover, just as there are crossover films, there are crossover cinemas, where many of the regular customers will pay to see arthouse films with quality production values as well as certain mainstream pictures. The development of multiplex cinemas across much of Europe has also increased the possibilities for flexible programming within a single cinema complex.[8]

> *"For all types of films, the distributor must book screens as far in advance as possible to allow time to implement an effective marketing plan."*

For all types of films, the distributor must book screens as far in advance as possible to allow time to implement an effective marketing plan. For mainstream films, distributors can generally book their dates and cinemas from three to six months in advance. In some territories (Greece, for example), bookings are made on a yearly basis. Potential blockbusters with name stars and directors, bought on script, can also be booked a year in advance.

In some cases, release dates are subject to modification, because exhibitors may decide to extend the run of a film that is performing particularly well. Such a film is known as a hold-over. As the result of a hold-over, the release of subsequent films may be pushed back, which may force a distributor to change such aspects of its marketing campaign as the timing of advertisements in newspapers and magazines at very short notice.

Distributors of specialized films prefer to book a picture into an exhibition schedule as far ahead of its release as possible. The early

---

[8] See Section 6 for more details.

booking of a release date is important because many of the magazines that provide important editorial coverage of specialized titles may have a three-month gap, which is known as "lead time," between their press deadline and their publication date. However, such distributors often face the problem of convincing an exhibitor of the commercial value of a specialized film. In many cases, the exhibitor will only be prepared to commit to a film after having seen it. Therefore, a distributor may wish to wait until a film has achieved box-office success in its country of origin or received some media exposure—for instance, through a film festival that provides press attention—before booking it.

When booking a specialized film, a distributor must constantly pressure exhibitors to convince them of that film's value and, thus, secure a strong release date. A distributor will strive at all times to cultivate the best possible personal relationships in the service of obtaining these dates. Most specialized films are booked into cinemas from two to five months ahead of their release dates. Arthouse cinemas tend to have rigid booking policies: a film will be booked for a four- or five-week run and, as long as it grosses more than the "house nut" (the cinema's weekly overhead costs), it will complete its run.

The interests of the exhibitor and the distributor are rather different, and this difference can lead to conflict, particularly in the case of pictures that do not perform as strongly as expected. If a film is significantly underperforming, the exhibitor will want to pull it off the screen as quickly as possible, but the distributor will want to extend its run to recover as much of its P&A costs as possible.

Distributors who also have interests in exhibition—such as Gaumont and UGC in France, Cecchi Gori in Italy, Lauren Films in Spain, and Kinowelt in Germany—are in a stronger position than most of their rivals when it comes to booking films because they have a much greater level of control over playdates. On occasion, this strength can create problems for other distributors because these distributor/exhibitors may be tempted to give their own films preferential treatment at the expense of films acquired from other parties.

To have more power vis-à-vis exhibitors and to guarantee playdates and available cinemas, some independent distributors have joined forces with some U.S. majors' distribution arms, which supervise the

108

MARKETING AND
SELLING
YOUR FILM
AROUND THE
WORLD

distribution of the independents' films–booking cinemas and collecting film-rental revenues–while the independents supervise marketing. For instance, Cinecompany sub-distributes pictures on behalf of 20th Century Fox in Spain.

■ Selecting a Release Date

Those responsible for planning a film's release date and release pattern can play a pivotal role in determining a film's box-office fate. Their decisions in these matters, along with the decisions of those who create a film's advertising and publicity campaign, may have considerable impact on a film's performance. If they make a misjudgment about the best release date or the required number of prints, even the strongest title can see its box-office performance suffer heavily.

The day of the week on which a film opens is usually determined by the accepted practice within a particular country. For instance, the opening day for films in France is Wednesday, but it is Thursday in Germany and Friday in the U.K., Italy, Spain, and the Scandinavian countries.

Three key factors influence the decision as to when to open a film:

Time of Year

The time of year when a film is to open must be considered very carefully, bearing in mind the rhythm of cinemagoing over the year. The frequency of cinemagoing in Europe is subject to strong seasonal fluctuations that are linked to the weather and to holiday periods. The yearly pattern of European cinemagoing may be broken down into three distinct periods:

> *"The time of year when a film is to open must be considered very carefully."*

• September through December
Cinemagoing is at its peak during this period, and is especially high over the Christmas holiday, when admissions may reach as high as thirty percent above average. (An exception is the U.K., which is more irregular.) During the holiday period, cinemagoing is a family event, so films aimed at children or young teenagers perform particularly strongly.

• January through April
Admissions remain strong, usually peaking over the Easter holiday. In Mediterranean countries, admissions may start to fall as early as April because, with the increase in temperature, people turn to outdoor leisure pursuits.

• May through August
This is usually considered the time of the year when the independent distributor faces the highest risks, particularly in the Mediterranean countries, where attendance levels can be heavily affected by the weather. Traditionally, large Hollywood films released by the U.S. majors have dominated the European box office during this period. Since such films often ride on the back of the vast publicity campaigns that accompanied their releases just a few weeks earlier in the U.S., weather fluctuations tend to have far less impact on their box-office performance in Europe.[9] Recent examples of summer successes include *Airbag*, which was released in Spain by Cinecompany and took in $8 million, becoming Spain's all-time top-grossing film, and *Men in Black*, which became the all-time biggest first-day opener in France in the Summer 1997.

In Germany, distributors launched a $20 million generic campaign in 1996 to counter the summer admissions drop. As a result, admissions increased by 62.5%.

Until the late 1980s, few European distributors were prepared to open potentially strong films during the summer months. But as multiplex cinemas have spread across Europe, and as exhibitors have

---

[9] In the U.S., the summer is one of the strongest periods for releasing films, particularly those aimed at the teenage market.

introduced air-conditioning into many older cinemas, summer weather has had less of an effect on attendance and independent distributors are prepared to open a much wider range of pictures during this period. Promotional initiatives that provide huge discounts on cinema tickets on certain days and allow the general public to meet directors and stars, such as the Fête du cinéma, held in France in late June, and the Festa del Cinema, held in Italy in May and June, have also helped boost summertime cinema attendance.[10]

Competition from Other Titles

The optimum opening dates for films will also be the most heavily booked dates. Distributors know in advance that their competitors will also play at the same time, so they can either decide to compete head to head or choose another date to open. Even varying a release by a single week can make a considerable difference in a film's box-office performance. This is particularly true for specialized titles that are likely to be heavily dependent on reviews. A distributor of such a film will try to ensure that it is the strongest release in a particular week, since this will help the picture secure a prominent position in a critic's review of the week's releases.

Generally, mainstream commercial films can be released at any time during the year, although they tend to monopolize the screens over holiday periods. Arthouse films need a longer run to increase and take advantage of word of mouth. Therefore, the less competitive times of the year (outside the holiday periods, for example) are often the best times for arthouse films to open.

Genre is another factor to be considered when choosing an opening date. If three strong action films and thrillers are being released, a smaller romantic movie or a comedy, released simultaneously, will offer the audience an alternative. For example, PolyGram Film Entertainment decided to launch the British comedy *Bean* in the Summer of 1997 because they knew that mostly disaster and science-fiction

---

[10] In France, the 1997 Fete du cinéma attracted some four million people, a fourteen percent increase over 1996.

movies were being released at the time. According to Jan Verheyen, head of international distribution for PFE, by the time *Bean* opened in the U.S. in November of 1997, it had already made over $100 million in Europe and Australasia. As this was very rare phenomenon, the film attracted a lot of interest from the trade press and the general media, and the $18 million comedy grossed another $43 million in the U.S. alone.

The technique of positioning a film so that it will offer an alternative to other films scheduled for release at a particular time is known as "counter-programming." An independent distributor's skillful use of counter-programming can offer a serious challenge to films with a much larger marketing budget.

Using Key Dates in the Film Calendar

The positioning of films around the Oscars and, to a lesser degree, film festivals, can have a significant impact on their box-office performance.

• The Oscars
European distributors with films that they feel are potential Oscar nominees will often try to hold back the release dates of these films until the Oscar nominations are unveiled in mid-February. In this way, such a film will open just as the nominations are announced, and, if the film is nominated, it should receive considerable publicity in the run-up to the event itself in late March. However, this strategy is something of a gamble: If the film is not nominated, the distributor may not be able to secure cinemas because the film will have lost one of its main marketing hooks, its nomination. And even if a cinema is secured for the film, it will then be competing with films that have been nominated. Alternatively, the distributor may release the film on a relatively small scale at an earlier date and broaden its release as the nominations are unveiled. In this way, the distributor will maximize the film's box-office potential.

An Oscar award can help a film attract significant additional audiences, and, as a result, distributors are often keen to re-release it as soon after the ceremony as possible.

• The Cannes Film Festival

The Cannes Film Festival is the most important international film festival, with around 3,500 accredited journalists covering both the festival and the market. The effects of the press reaction to a film can extend far beyond the event itself, and the impact of reviews at Cannes can frequently offer a stark demonstration of the power of the media.

With such extensive free publicity surrounding the screening of a film, distributors often exploit the publicity generated by the film at the festival and launch the film at the same time in its home territory. Its release date can be set for a time during the festival, preferably before the awards ceremony or before the festival screening of the film.[11]

Because of the intensity of the media attention focused on Cannes, and the fact that the critics view an enormous number of films within a very short space of time there, the media reaction to films often swings between the extremes of extravagant praise and extreme hostility. The domestic box-office performance of a film will often benefit from the impact of a favorable response at Cannes. Equally, however, poor reviews from Cannes can often destroy the box-office potential of a picture.

For a small film that is entirely dependent on reviews, an excellent response at Cannes can be enormously beneficial. In many cases, the press reaction at Cannes can have a more significant effect on the fate of a film than the official awards. However, there are no firm rules governing this relationship. Quentin Tarantino's *Pulp Fiction* achieved significant extra box-office as a result of winning the Palme d'Or in 1994, while the Palme d'Or had very little impact on the international box-office revenues of the Swedish film *The Best Intentions*, which won in 1992. As stressed by PolyGram's Jan Verheyen, for the Palme d'Or

---

[11] Films cannot be entered for the official competition at Cannes if they have been released outside their national territory.

to have any impact on a film's box-office revenues, that film has to be somehow "user friendly."

■ The Release

A film's release pattern can be as crucial as its release date in determining that film's box-office success. The factors that a distributor will assess when considering a film's release pattern are the number of prints in which the film will be released, the towns and cities where the film will play, and the specific cinemas in which the film will be released.

> *" A film's release pattern can be as crucial as its release date in determining that film's box-office success. "*

Two release patterns exist:

Day-and-Date Release

With a "day-and-date" release, a distributor releases a film on the same day throughout a given country, generally with the maximum number of prints. A "wide-opening" release also utilizes the maximum number of prints, although the release dates are staggered, starting with key cities. Both techniques are used

> *" If a day-and-date release does not open well, its box-office recovery is usually very difficult. "*

for mainstream commercial pictures, and are designed to create the maximum public awareness possible during a film's opening week or weekend and to take advantage of a large advertising spend timed to coincide with the opening date.

A strong opening is essential to sustain a film's life because, during a film's first week, its exhibitor will decide to keep it or not. If a day-and-date release does not open well, its box-office recovery is usually very difficult. A day-and-date release will be backed up by an extensive advertising and publicity campaign. However, a day-and-date release often shortens a film's life and accelerates the rotation of films on screen because each film usually has a limited audience demand.

The stakes for a day-and-date release are high, especially for the independent distributor. A successful day-and-date release should ensure a relatively quick passage of substantial revenues from exhibitor to producer. A failure, however, can be disastrous because it will often shorten the life of a film that has very high P&A costs. However, on a film that is expected to perform poorly over time, a day-and-date release can be advantageous because it can enable it to gross a lot in its first week—before negative word-of-mouth starts to circulate among its potential audience.

The scale of a day-and-date release differs according to the type of film being released and the marketplace. A blockbuster from a U.S. major can go out with over a thousand prints in Germany, 600 in France, and 200 in Spain. Large independent distributors can also afford similar saturation releases for mainstream films featuring major stars, although the cost of prints may sometimes act as a deterrent.

Platform Release

With a "platform" release, the number of initial prints is limited, and a distributor may open a film on only one or a limited number of screens is one key city and then, after one or two weeks, expand its opening to more screens and more cities. A platform release is often used for specialized films that need a long run to develop word-of-mouth. In many ways, such a release is much harder to plan than a mainstream film's wider release because audience targeting for a platform release can be particularly tricky. With a platform release, creativity and an understanding of the film's potential audience can be as important as the amount of money available to market and promote it.

Properly targeting the city where a platform release will open is vital. In capital cities, where a greater number of cinemas provide a greater programming diversity and adult audiences have increased access to quality films, a greater film awareness exists. Also, a higher level of disposable income is usually available to cinemagoers in these cities.

A mainstream commercial film can be platformed in a cinema in a capital city in any given country during its first week of release, or for several weeks, in the hope that media coverage, which tends to be concentrated in such cities, will boost that film's profile before it goes nationwide.

A specialized film can be platformed with one print in an exclusive run, or with several prints at a small number of prestige houses (e.g., the Curzon Mayfair and the Gate in London). If a film is shown in only one cinema, the distributor is effectively emphasizing the picture's exclusivity. Platforming a film in several cinemas conveys to the audience the notion that the film is a quality picture, but also amortizes the distributor's advertising and public relations expenditures across a number of screens.

In the U.K., most specialized or arthouse films open in London, followed by release in the provinces anywhere from two to six weeks later. In Spain, such pictures would typically open in Madrid and Barcelona before being released in other cities. In Italy, a platform release will often open in Rome and Milan, and a few weeks later the release will be widened to include such cities as Florence, Bologna, and Naples. In Germany, the consensus is that there are seven key cities: Berlin, Hamburg, Munich, Frankfurt, Düsseldorf, Stuttgart, and Cologne. (The key cities in Europe are shown in the accompanying chart.) Box-office receipts in London and Paris, for example, and several other key European cities act as indicators of a film's likely overall box office within specific territories. After opening in these key cities, a film will be released to a second wave of smaller cities, and then to a third wave of minor cities and towns.

Determining the optimum strategy for a film's platform release requires the distributor to balance the most effective means of targeting an audience against the costs involved in doing so. It is wise not to overspend at the beginning of a platform release campaign because maintaining the public's interest and slowly building an audience through release advertising (often using quotes from favorable reviews) is important.

Key European cities for the relase of films

BELGIUM	Brussels, Liege, Antwerp, Ghent
DENMARK	Copenhagen, Aarhus
FRANCE	Paris, Marseille, Bordeaux, Toulouse, Metz, Lille, Rouen, Nancy, Nice, Lyon, Strasbourg, Grenoble
GERMANY	Berlin, Cologne, Hamburg, Munich, Frankfurt, Dusseldorf, Stuttgart, Dresden, Leipzig, Erfurt
GREECE	Athens, Salonica, Patras
IRELAND	Dublin, Cork
ITALY	Rome, Milan, Florence, Bologna, Naples, Padua, Bari, Calgari, Catania
LUXEMBOURG	Luxembourg
NETHERLANDS	Amsterdam, Rotterdam, The Hague, Utrecht
PORTUGAL	Lisbon, Oporto
SPAIN	Madrid, Barcelona, Seville, Bilbao, Valencia, Zaragoza
U.K.	London, Edinburgh, Glasgow, Newcastle, Manchester, Brighton, Liverpool, Birmingham, Cardiff, Oxford, Southampton, Cambridge,

However, the distributor must spend a sufficient amount of money to allow the various elements of the marketing campaign—advertising, publicity, and promotion—to have an impact. One advertisement or interview is not enough to create awareness, let alone want-to-see. Awareness of a film must be reinforced over a period of several weeks. This is where the media will play a major role.

The sheer costs of P&A can make it uneconomic to open with a very small number of prints because the costs of producing marketing materials (posters and trailers), advertising, and merchandising are normally fixed, regardless of whether a film is released with five prints or 500 prints. Therefore, to recoup one's investment in marketing, advertising, and merchandising, one would wish to go out with enough prints to maximize an opening weekend's potential while keeping an eye on building toward future playdates.

While a film's playdate and the release pattern are set, the tools that will be used to position the film for its target audience are developed and a strategy for the use of these tools is put in place.

■ The Prints and Advertising Budget

Determining the most effective P&A budget for a film is one of the most critical parts of the marketing process. Without an adequate budget, the likelihood that a film will reach its target audience is greatly reduced.

The cost of prints, advertising, publicity, promotion, and sometimes market research make up a film's P&A budget. The main items of expenditure in a P&A budget are

Print costs, including

• Subtitling or dubbing, if a film is in a foreign language and is not going to be shown in its original version.

• Accessing or buying an inter-negative from which to make the required number of prints.

• Production of the prints themselves, known as feature prints, plus the duplication of any trailer prints.

• Shipping costs and the duty payable on prints and materials imported from abroad.

• Costs that are sometimes incurred because of the necessity of re-cutting a film to meet a particular country's censorship requirements.

Advertising costs, including

• Designing and printing posters for display in cinemas and on billboards.

• Creating trailers, which will run prior to a film's release.

• Advertising space in newspapers and magazines.

• Advertising spots on radio.

• Advertising time on television.

• Advertising within cinemas.

• Outdoor advertising (on billboards, buses, trains, and whatever else will stay still long enough to accept the application of a poster or a flyer).

Publicity costs, including

• Stills (black-and-white) for distribution to media.

• Transparencies (color) for distribution to media.

• Electronic press kits (EPKs) for television and radio.

• Other press kits for printed media.

• One-sheets (industry-standard 40-inch x 27-inch posters) for distribution to the media and/or the general public.

• Pre-release press screenings of a film for the media (for review purposes and to spread awareness of a film).

• Press attaché to secure media coverage.

• Special stills of stars and/or the director that are purchased from outside parties or shot at special photo shoots.

Promotional costs, including

• Merchandising, such as the production of promotional toys or free gifts.

• Tie-ins, such as competitions arranged in conjunction with radio stations and retail outlets.

• Advance screenings, which are set up in advance of the official release and designed to spread awareness of a film through word-of-mouth.

The P&A budget is often contractually fixed with a distributor and a sales agent or a producer, with specified minimum and maximum spending limitations. Its costs are generally borne by the distributor.

"The P&A budget is often contractually fixed with a distributor and a sales agent or a producer, with specified minimum and maximum spending limitations."

Once a film is released, and subject to a sales agreement with the producer or sales representative, P&A costs will be deducted before the producers' share is calculated, but after the distributor has taken a commission fee and deducted release costs. This type of deal, known as cost off the top (COT), is most common when a distributor has paid an up-front minimum guarantee to a sales agent for the right to distribute a film in a certain territory for a specified length of time.[12]

If a minimum guarantee has not been advanced, the distributor will usually participate in the first receipts, alongside the producer, after the exhibitor's share has been deducted. In this type of deal, a gross deal, the distributor will take a much higher percentage—up to seventy to eighty percent of the total—because P&A costs have to be recouped from these receipts. Once P&A costs are recouped by the distributor, the percentage split of receipts between the producer and the distributor will usually be set at fifty-fifty.

In many cases, the amount spent on P&A in a particular territory may equal the minimum guarantee for a film. If, for example, the minimum guarantee put up by a U.K. distributor is $100,000, this will often mean that that same amount of money will be spent on P&A. The film would then have to generate between $300,000 to $400,000 gross at the box office (allowing for deductions, including Value Added Tax (VAT), and the exhibitor's share) for the distributor to break even.[13] Assuming that the picture grosses this amount, the twenty-five percent remitted to the distributor is the net rental.

---

[12] See Section 3, International Sales.

[13] Value Added Tax is a European tax, similar to a federal sales tax, that is applied to certain goods in each country. VAT is not charged on tickets in some European territories.

After the distributor has taken a share of the net rentals, the remainder will be split between the sales agent and the producer, according to a previously agreed formula, which will usually vary from picture to picture.

A film's marketing budget is usually calculated in terms of its projected box-office and likely performance in ancillary media. The likely box-office for a mainstream film is usually calculated on the basis of the past performances of similar films. But such comparisons must always be treated with caution, given the singular nature of each film and its dependence on such factors as the effectiveness of its advertising campaign and word-of-mouth.

When calculating the appropriate P&A budget for a film, some distributors include the amount of potential revenue that can be anticipated from video and television distribution, as well as the expected theatrical gross. The revenues that are expected to be generated by video and television can be set against the P&A budget in this way because the theatrical marketing campaign will serve as a showcase for the film, ensuring that most consumers are aware of the title when it is released in ancillary media. The value of a theatrical marketing campaign is therefore not restricted to cinema exhibition alone, but may have a considerable effect on video sales and a film's value for television sales.

P&A Costs in Europe

P&A costs vary widely from country to country, depending on the size of the market and the possibilities of recouping these costs from theatrical, television, and video releases.

Generally speaking, release costs have spiraled during the past fifteen years. In Europe, although no accurate figures exist to document the trend, it is widely accepted that P&A costs have risen sharply—tripled over the past seven years, according to some industry experts—primarily as a result of the rising costs of advertising. In the U.S., the rise in P&A costs has been even more dramatic and, on average, studios spend almost half of a film's budget on P&A.[14]

---

[14] According to figures from the Motion Picture Association of America, the average cost of a film released by a major Hollywood studio in 1997 was $75.6 million, a 26.6% rise from 1996's average. That $75.6 million includes average marketing costs of $22.2 million (a 12.2% rise from the previous year).

With P&A costs soaring, cinema admissions falling in many territories, and total revenues concentrated on a smaller number of films, the risks for the independent distributor in Europe have increased considerably.

For commercial reasons, the precise marketing costs for specific films tend to be a closely guarded secrets and distributors are reluctant to divulge exact P&A expenditures. The practice of discounting rate-card prices for advertising media, which is particularly prevalent in such countries as France and Spain, and the prevalence of volume discounts obtained from servicing companies in return for guaranteeing them a certain level of work, makes the exact calculation of these costs particularly difficult. Obtaining reliable P&A costs is further complicated by the fact that while some costs, such as those of prints, tend to be fixed, the prices of other items, such as dubbing, can vary enormously from country to country. (See Dubbing and Subtitling Costs below.)

Even when it is possible to obtain figures on P&A costs, these may not include hidden discounts on advertisement space or rebates from film laboratories. Because of such hidden elements, sales agents often insist on receiving a minimum guarantee from a distributor, because this assures them that they should receive some money back from a film's distribution rather than seeing all the revenues absorbed by an artificially inflated P&A budget.

Dubbing and Subtitling Costs

All films that are not shot in a language native to the specific territory where they are to be released will need to be dubbed or subtitled. The cost of this will form part of the P&A budget. While a good dub or an excellent subtitling will not be sufficient to rescue a poor film, poor dubbing or indifferent subtitling can certainly hamper the performance of any film. Too often, distributors allocate insufficient money for this purpose and sales agents or producers deliver inferior materials, such as poor-quality magnetic soundtracks, which can delay a film's eventual release, lead to increased costs, and adversely effect a film's box-office potential.

In some European territories, the practice of dubbing prevails; in others, subtitling is preferred. In Europe, films are most often dubbed in Italy, France, Spain, and Germany, for both cultural and economic reasons. However, in France, Spain, and Germany subtitled versions of films are generally used in their key cities' arthouse cinemas. (A subtitled print is referred to as an "Original Version" in newspaper listings.) In the smaller territories, such as the Benelux countries, Greece, and Portugal, the costs of dubbing are prohibitive, so subtitling is the norm. In such countries, the dominance of English-language films is even greater than in countries where dubbing prevails.

Dubbing prices vary considerably according to the length and amount of dialogue in a film, but the same original dialogue, when dubbed in various different countries, will also show broad, country-to-country cost variations. For example, dubbing in Italy is particularly expensive because of the economic demands of Italian actors' unions. However, such costs are amortized across ancillary media as well as on the theatrical release.

A distributor will take four to six weeks to prepare a film's foreign version, and will need quality subtitled or dubbed prints to use in media screenings four to six months in advance of the film's release. If the critics are obliged to base their review on a poorly dubbed or subtitled version of a film, this may adversely affect their opinions of the picture. Therefore, the distributor must secure a print from the sales agent or producer as early as possible. The earlier a film is available for subtitling or dubbing, the better the chances of quality results.

Independent distribution in Europe is a high-risk business. As an increased share of the box office is claimed by the U.S. majors and P&A costs rise, independents find themselves increasingly squeezed by economic pressures. The limited P&A resources available to European independent distributors has had the effect of making them work particularly hard to maximize creativity and cost-effectiveness.

Once a P&A budget has been set, a distributor must determine the most effective way to spend that money, with the goal of attracting the largest possible audience for the picture.

■ The Essential Ingredients of an Advertising Campaign

In addition to choosing the best release date for a film and making sure that it is available to as many targeted cinemas as possible, a distributor's skill lies in his ability to increase awareness of a film and fire an audience's desire to see it. The usual means to achieve these goals are through advertising, publicity, and promotion.

For mainstream films, advance advertising often creates the highest levels of awareness, interest, and want-to-see. A specialized film's distributor will rely less on advance advertising and concentrate more on the film's release and post-release periods to encourage word of mouth and try to convince exhibitors to keep playing the film.

The following section will examine the creation and use of marketing materials, starting with the materials used in paid advertising. It will then move on to consider the role of publicity and promotion in the distribution campaign.

Overall Planning

Given that a distributor's goal is to market a picture to the general public, when compared with a film's producer or director, a distributor may have a strategic advantage when it comes to designing a film's marketing tools. A distributor that has a knowledge of the marketplace is arguably better positioned than a producer or a director to create a poster and a trailer that will be effective

" A distributor that has a knowledge of the marketplace is arguably better positioned than a producer or a director to create a poster and a trailer that will be effective in attracting a film's target audience. "

124

MARKETING AND
SELLING
YOUR FILM
AROUND THE
WORLD

in attracting a film's target audience. A film's director and its producer are primarily concerned with realizing their vision of the film, and may simply be too close to the project to be able to conceive the most effective way of attracting the general public, although their input into this process can still be extremely useful.

If a film's distribution deal is in place before production starts, the distributor's marketing department will usually develop its marketing tools together with the producer and the director. In this instance, the available materials will often be adapted to market needs right from the inception of the project. The distributor will subsequently hire creative agencies (to design a poster and make a trailer) and advertising agencies (to book advertising space), which will usually employ ideas based on the distributor's marketing brief. These agencies will often work closely with either the distributor's in-house public relations agent or a public relations agency specifically hired to help market the film. But since the distributor is paying the bills, the distributor will maintain final control of the campaign.

Most European distributors stress that producers should always include the costs of basic marketing materials in their initial production budget. This will save time and money and improve the quality of the promotional material produced. Without a unit publicist and photographer working on marketing material during production, the distributor will have to invest far more in P&A for the film at its release stage, when it will then be more expensive to secure special shots of the cast or the director.

Photographs

For European distributors, photographs will form a crucial part of their advertising campaign. Photographs, which can be used in posters and distributed to the press, are vital for creating a film's visual image, because few distributors are able to afford television advertising.[15] As

---

[15] In France, marketing practices are very different from other territories because the advertising of films on television is not permitted. This advertising ban was introduced about thirty years ago to curb the powers of broadcasters and major theatrical distributors.

has been stressed earlier in this book, before the start of a film's principal photography, the producer and the distributor should ensure that they can secure high-quality black-and-white and color photographs while the film is shooting. After a film's principal photography is finished, trying to shoot photographs of the cast will be considerably more difficult and costly. Wherever possible, the distributor should hire a professional unit photographer who will shoot from a brief provided by the producer, the distributor, or the unit publicist. Since color photos can be converted to black-and-white, shooting sixty percent of the photographs in color and forty percent in black-and-white is usually advisable.

Creating the Poster Art

In Europe, particularly in France, where the qualitative aspect of a marketing campaign is more important than the quantitative, the poster is the primary medium for advertising a film. Since the poster focuses a wide audience's attention on a specific film, the message it is likely to convey to the audience needs to be studied carefully. The process of creating a poster for a film's public distribution is broadly similar to that described for creating posters to support a film's international presales (as outlined in Section 4, Markets and Festivals).

The percentage of a film's marketing budget that is spent on producing a poster is relatively low in terms of the total P&A. However, the purchasing of space for displaying posters will constitute a more significant budget item. But, since the poster will also form the basis of a film's print advertisements, its importance cannot be underestimated, and distributors must ensure that they invest wisely to secure the most effective images for their films.

A distributor will often have a specific conception on how to position a film for its audience, and will work closely with designers to ensure that this conception is realized. In the first stage of a film's poster development, the distributor and the in-house creative personnel meet with the advertising agencies and the various designers that have been retained to create the film's advertising visuals. All those involved are shown a rough cut of the film, or the completed film if a print is available. If no footage is available, the designers will work from the script and any photographs that are available from the shoot.

In Europe, some distributors are not afraid of hiring a pool of designers to develop as many as thirty or forty different visual images while the distributor attempts to find the campaign that has the best possible chance of maximizing a particular film's audience.

As a result of cost constraints, some European distributors choose to adapt a film's original poster campaign, which was created in the country where the film originated, to their local market. If they are generally satisfied with the material provided by the producer or the sales agent, they may simply make slight modifications to it, such as adding taglines in the local language. In some cases, the same basic poster may be used across many different territories. But the different poster formats used in various European territories can still create additional printing costs for the distributor.

In the case of mainstream pictures handled by the U.S. majors, the same campaign will often be used across most of the territories in which a film is released. This is largely a testament to the power of the Hollywood marketing machine whose norms and values are familiar to audiences throughout the world. But with international box-office receipts often exceeding those earned in the U.S. and marketing becoming more complex in many overseas territories, U.S. studios are increasingly using local adaptations.

London is an important center for the production of marketing materials because it is where many of the largest international sales companies are based.[16] Paris is another important center for postermaking because it is the biggest film capital in Europe and the French prohibition of television advertising for films has underlined the poster's importance as an advertising medium. In France, however, the total cost of creating a poster is much higher than in the U.K.: Posters that cost from $5,000 to $10,000 in the U.K. will cost from $6,500 to $49,000 in France, the highest range being for artworks signed by famous artists. The importance of these two centers—London

---

[16] See Section 3, International Sales.

and Paris–is further reflected in the fact that English and French poster campaigns are often re-used throughout Europe.

Poster artwork can include illustrations, photographs, and graphics. If there are no production stills to work with, designers using computer graphics can combine images from photo libraries into a montage, although this will add to a poster's cost.

Creating the Copy for the Poster

The copy is the text on a film's poster that, in conjunction with the visual image, plays a vital role in selling a film to its audience. The copy helps cinemagoers relate to a film by highlighting the names of its stars and its director and its other relevant elements.

In some European territories, poster copy will often consist of taglines that emphasize a particular aspect of a film's story, certain awards that it has won, or the track record of its director and stars. The use of taglines tends to be more prevalent in northern Europe.

Taglines will usually highlight the following:

• The dramatic elements of the story, which might include love, danger, adventure, mystery, etc. For example, the U.K. poster for *As Good as It Gets* read, "A comedy about truth, justice and other special effects." For *Gattaca*, it read, "There is no gene for the human spirit." For *Titanic*, the poster read, "Nothing on Earth Could Come Between Them." For *I Know What You Did Last Summer*, it read, "If you are going to bury the truth, make sure it stays buried."

• Awards. On posters for films that have won a prize in Cannes, Venice, or Berlin, the particular award's logo may be featured or the text may mention prizes won by the director and/or the cast.

• The stars or director. Previous films from particular director or that feature specific stars will be mentioned if they have achieved box-office success. For example, the tagline on the U.K. poster for Jim Sheridan's *The Boxer* read, "From the acclaimed director of *My Left Foot* and *In the Name of the Father*." The tagline for Wim Wenders' *The End of Violence* read, "From the director of *Wings of Desire* and *Paris, Texas*."

In some European countries, poster copy may also feature quotes from critics, praising particular aspects of a film or its overall entertainment value. Such a quote's source, not just its nature, is important in determining its effectiveness. For instance, with a mainstream commercial picture, a distributor will usually try to use quotes from mass-circulation newspapers because these quotes will constitute the best stamp of approval for that film's target audience. For an arthouse film, positive reviews by critics from quality newspapers or magazines can have a decisive impact on the film's potential audience. A film's visuals, along with these quotes, are then placed in key newspapers and magazines that target the appropriate audience and/or used as display or one-sheet advertisements in cinema lobbies.

Since an audience may weigh the merits of one film against another on the basis of their posters, it is arguable that the absence of taglines or copy quotes on film posters in certain countries may hurt the effectiveness of a film's marketing campaign.

The billing on a poster lists the talent (producer, director, stars) and the crew that contributed to the film's production. A distributor's designers are often under contractual obligation as to the positioning and size of the names that appear on any promotional material. The larger the film, the more specific such obligations will be. For instance, the names of certain famous cast members may have to appear on the poster in a size that is at least twenty-five percent of the size of the title and also be placed in a specific position.

Positioning the Poster

Most posters are used at outdoor sites, although some will also be displayed in cinemas. Expenditure on outdoor posters in Europe is relatively high–in France, for example, posters may account for as much as fifty-eight percent of a film's total advertising budget, while in the U.S., expenditure on outdoor posters often represents less than one percent, and in the U.K., less than five percent.

A poster campaign will generally start two weeks before a film's release and continue during its first week of the release. To maximize the effect of poster advertising, distributors often complement this campaign with fly-posting, the unofficially posting of posters on walls and buildings.

" Outdoor posters can be highly cost effective. "

Outdoor posters can be highly cost effective because they usually reach the core cinemagoing audience (urban, ages fifteen through thirty-five) who use public transport every day. Outdoor posters can also be used at strategic sites close to cinemas. Furthermore, by using the same visual material on a film's posters and advertisements and in cinema foyers, a high level of audience awareness of a particular film can be achieved.

Although outdoor posters can be placed in specific geographical areas, the targeting of a specific audience remains relatively inexact because such billboards mainly reach mass urban audiences that are difficult to place in subgroups. In the major European cities, positions for outdoor posters include underground trains, buses, bus shelters, and roadside billboards.

In each European country, poster spaces will be booked through a national or a local sales house or through an advertising agency. In some countries, such as France, a relatively limited amount of poster space is available because of the high level of competition between distributors. This means that such bookings have to be made anywhere from four to twelve months in advance of a film's release. This can create problems for independent distribution companies that have little power over the release dates of their films. Although it is still possible to strike deals at the last minute, such arrangements may not always allow sufficient time for a poster to be printed.

The high degree of competition for outdoor sites in France has led sales houses to offer new types of sites. For example, Metrobus, the advertising sales house for the public transport company RATP, sells spaces on handrails and entry doors in their underground railway system. These are ideal locations because they are relatively inexpensive and enjoy is a high volume of pedestrian traffic.

In the cinemas, posters will be highly visible. The advantage of positioning posters in cinemas is that they will always reach the cinemagoer.

For a major release, a teaser poster is often created to precede the appearance of a main poster. A teaser poster usually presents just a few of a film's details (perhaps its title, its tagline, and its opening date). These posters are designed to incite an audience's interest in seeking more information about a film. If a teaser poster campaign is used, it will usually start four to five weeks before a film's release.

Censorship

In each European territory, local authorities or national film censorship boards may have the statutory right to review marketing materials to determine whether they are deemed likely to cause public offense. When distributors create marketing campaigns, they must bear in mind the possibility of censorship. For example, in the U.K., where censorship is particularly strict, posters showing guns pointing at people or men looming over women are prohibited. The London Transport Authority, which operates the city's buses and underground railways, will expect to see the artwork that is to be put up on its billboards to advertise any film that is restricted to cinemagoers who are over the age of eighteen.

Creating and Using the Trailer

A film's trailer can be one of its most effective marketing tools because it directly addresses the cinemagoer. A trailer is usually the first sales tool to appear, preceding a film's poster and other forms of advertising. Unlike other forms of advertising, a trailer allows an audience to sample a film directly, a fact that enhances its importance. As a consequence, a trailer can play a crucial factor in determining an audience's response to a film. Ideally, a trailer should first play in the cinema around six weeks before a film's release and keep playing until the picture opens.

" Unlike other forms of advertising, a trailer allows an audience to sample a film directly. "

A trailer has four main functions:

1) To create awareness of a film's title.

2) To impart an overall impression of a film to its potential audience.

3) To ensure that a film's potential audience is aware of the film's director and main stars (in cases where such names will help sell a picture).

4) To create want-to-see among the potential audience.

Trailers are made by specialist companies and usually take between six and eight weeks to complete. A trailer company will usually work in consultation with a film's producer, director, distributor, and, where relevant, sales agent–seeking to identify those marketable elements of a film that will make the most effective trailer. Unlike posters, trailers are usually not constrained by contractual obligations, although, in certain cases, the director may have the right of approval over the trailer.

Trailers for certain types of films–such as those with crossover potential–will attempt to appeal to multiple segments of the audience. For example, the campaigns for certain male-oriented films may need to be constructed in such a way that these pictures have some appeal to (or, at least, do not completely repel) females who might accompany the target male audience to the cinema.

A trailer is usually cut from a film's release print and will require both a script and music. The ideal length for a trailer is between 90 and 120 seconds. If it is any longer, exhibitors may be reluctant to play it. For big releases, a distributor usually makes three or four trailers for every film print.

When European distributors handle U.S. films, they usually adapt the existing U.S. trailer campaign in some way. Re-editing will often be used to tone down such a trailer because U.S. trailers often tend to use a hard-sell approach with fast cuts and the repetition of key scenes from the film. A U.S. trailer may also be re-voiced and adjusted for length.

Teaser Trailers

Teaser trailers use a combination of a film's footage, still photography, and graphics to give a very brief glimpse of a film with the goal of arousing an audience's curiosity. The ideal length for a teaser trailer is around thirty seconds, because this length gives it a strong chance of being inserted in an exhibitor's trailer reel.

Teasers will usually only be produced for mainstream films that will have a wide release backed by a high P&A budget. A teaser trailer should ideally start to play two to three months before a film's release. For blockbuster films from the U.S. majors, a teaser trailer might play as early as six months in advance of a film's release.

Getting the Trailer Played

Even a first-class trailer is useless if it does not play regularly in the cinema. Differences in the perceived value of trailers are a constant source of tension between distributors and exhibitors. Many distributors feel that exhibitors do not give sufficient emphasis to trailers. The distributor's responsibility is to ensure that trailers are played because no formal trailer contract with the exhibitor will exist.

> *" Even a first-class trailer is useless if it does not play regularly in the cinema. "*

Exhibitors usually play trailers in batches of three or four. They often sacrifice playing more trailers in favor of increasing their time for screen advertising for such goods as clothing, food, drinks, etc. The exhibitors' argument is that they do not directly benefit from trailers, unlike screen advertising, which provides them with an important source of revenue. To compensate for not playing trailers on screen, some exhibitors are now playing them on video monitors in their cinema foyers.

Certain exhibition companies that are owned by groups with interests in distribution may give preference to trailers that advertise films being handled by the distributors to which they are tied. This practice can cause difficulties for independent distributors that wish to place their trailers in such cinemas. If a distributor cannot get a trailer to play, it may be obliged to buy screen-advertising time from one of the companies responsible for selling it. Although this may be expensive, it will guarantee that a film's trailer is shown to its targeted audience. A screen-advertising booking company will target a trailer for showing in certain geographical zones (national, regional, or local cinemas), in particular types of cinemas, or with specific films.

The positioning of a trailer in the right cinema at the right time is as important as the positioning of the print itself. Trailers are usually played alongside films of a style or genre similar to that of the film being trailed. However, if a particular film is felt to have great cross-over potential, some audience-broadening advantages may be gained by screening its trailer before films of a rather different type.

As with so many aspects of the marketing process, timing is crucial: A very effective trailer that is delivered late or not at all is useless. Equally, distributors may need to exercise negotiating muscle with reluctant exhibitors to ensure that their trailers are played.

Creating and Using Press Advertising

In Europe, press advertising is an important means for informing the audience about when and where a film will play. After a film's release, newspaper advertising can reinforce its level of awareness and want-to-see. The primary medium for press advertising is newspapers, although film and entertainment magazines and other publications may also be used, depending on the target audience.

A print media advertising campaign usually starts two weeks prior to a film's opening. This campaign will usually draw on a film's poster for its visual images and include quotes from selected reviews in some territories, especially in northern Europe. A portion of a film's press advertising spend should be budgeted to help sustain word-of-mouth after a film's initial opening.

Teaser advertising campaigns, which use just a few of a film's details, may start anywhere from three to four weeks before a film's opening. Such teaser campaigns can be an effective way of igniting audience expectation.

Press advertising has the advantage of short lead times—for daily and weekly publications, advertisements can usually be booked just a few days in advance—but its impact is short-lived, especially in the case of daily publications. However, press advertising is still very popular in the U.K., where it almost equals television advertising.

The current decline in expenditure on print advertising can be ascribed to the changing nature of the relationship between distributors and the print media in recent years. Increasingly, distributors are striking promotional deals with the press, giving away cinema seats in return for free advertising space.

Creating and Using Websites

The use of websites has become an important marketing tool for many feature films. Depending on the sophistication of the website itself (straight information, computer games derived from the film, downloadable stills from the film, downloadable trailers or clips from the film), the costs for setting up a site can vary but would start at approximately $10,000.

Although websites cannot be targeted to specific audiences as direct-mail or specific newspaper advertising can be, for those who are computer literate and interested in film, an ever-expanding number of sites are readily accessible. These include film festival sites, film distributor sites, sites devoted to particular film genres, and sites devoted to directors and actors. For example, Sony Picture Entertainment has created several websites, including one dedicated to a SPE newsletter that contains film and television updates.

Through websites, reviews, and box-office information, especially from America (which can have an impact on global box-office results), is no longer restricted to what cinemagoers encounter in their local media. The instant access and awareness created by the Internet means that cinemagoers with the time and inclination to sift through the Web can be more aware of upcoming films than ever before. For distributors, creating advance awareness is an essential ingredient in their release strategies and the Internet is but another medium in which to generate information about their upcoming releases.

Creating and Using Television Advertising

The same companies that make trailers often also specialize in creating television campaigns for feature films. However, because of the extremely high costs of purchasing airtime, television advertising is usually only employed for high-budget films.

A television spot is usually between ten and thirty seconds in length. It is often a shortened version of the trailer, and it follows the trailer's production procedures: scripting, selecting, and editing. Note that the voice-over for a television spot can be particularly expensive.

A television campaign is usually timed to start five to ten days before a film opens, and if a picture is performing strongly, it may be continued during the film's first week of release.

In Europe, television advertising is used much less than it is in the U.S., primarily because of its high costs. In many cases, the high costs of television airtime means that European distributors may find it more cost-effective to invest in electronic press kits that can be shown free of charge during news or entertainment programs.

As mentioned earlier, the television advertising of theatrical movies has been banned in France since 1969. The film industry originally supported the ban because it was partly aimed at curbing the power of the broadcasters and of the major theatrical distributors–the only groups who could afford it. Negotiations to lift the ban are currently underway because the ban is now seen as an impediment to many marketing campaigns.

" Television advertising of theatrical movies has been banned in France since 1969. "

Television advertising for films is most common in Germany, Italy, and the U.K. In Italy, if the state broadcaster, RAI, has co-produced a film, or bought the television rights to it, it will usually offer discounted advertising time for the picture.

Satellite television is also increasingly being used in Europe as an advertising medium for mainstream releases. Many satellite channels are aimed at specific segments of the population and, therefore, offer distributors a chance to reach targeted audiences.

Creating and Using Radio Advertising

A film's radio campaign will often be created by the same company that created its trailer. For radio, the ideal advertising slot is about thirty seconds, although shorter spots of ten to fifteen seconds may also be produced. Radio advertising is usually used to increase awareness of and interest in a film during the run-up to its opening and during the first weeks of its release. A film's first radio spots will usually air two to three days in advance of its release. For large campaigns, radio ads are often used simultaneously with television ads as a means to reinforce good reviews if a film has opened well.

For campaigns with restricted budgets, radio spots offer an attractive alternative to television spots because they are cheaper. Radio is also an ideal medium for targeting particular groups, because many stations are aimed at specific segments of the population. For this reason, choosing the right slot on the right station is vital to reaching a film's targeted audience.

Radio can prove extremely valuable for films that have a strong soundtrack. Radio can also be particularly effective for youth-oriented films because teenagers tend to spend a relatively large amount of time listening to radio. For specialized films, radio spots are often too expensive, but distributors of such films have increasing access to discounts as part of promotional deals with radio stations.

Market Research

One method of testing the likely impact of a particular marketing strategy is market research. This can help assess whether a film has been positioned in a way that is likely to appeal to its potential audience.

Most commonly used in the U.S., market research is perceived as a quasi-scientific tool and used to gain a comprehensive knowledge of the state of the marketplace as well as to test the appeal of a film's elements—ranging from story content to the nature of the marketing campaign. It is thus very useful for assessing the potential effectiveness of posters and trailers prior to their release and helping a distributor determine the most effective means of positioning a film.

> *"One method of testing the likely impact of a particular marketing strategy is market research."*

Although an increasing number of European distributors are using market research, in particular for films with a medium budget, some in Europe remain suspicious of such techniques.

Market research findings are used to assess the following factors, some of which have been discussed in a different context earlier in this section:[17]

Playability

How do audiences respond to the film after having seen it? Do they like it? Will they recommend it to their friends? Which types of filmgoers, based on demographic and lifestyle attributes, rate it best? Are these groups large enough to open the picture, and will their word-of-mouth be credible?

Positioning

Which, of all the possible ways of selling the film, including combining different major and minor storylines, characters, and personnel (including actors, directors, screenwriters, and producers), gives the film an appeal to the widest audience? Does the target audience coincide with the types of filmgoers who rate the picture the highest? Is there a discrepancy between the playability and the marketability of the film? If so, how can this be resolved?

---

[17] This section was developed from material kindly supplied by Dr. Joseph Helfgot, president of Marketcast, a U.S.-based company specialising in market research for the film industry.

Marketing Materials

What specific marketing materials (posters, trailers, print ads, promotional campaigns) need to be developed to reflect the most successful positioning strategy for the film? Do these stimulate the desire to see the film?

Release Date

What release date will work best for a specific film, given the competition from other films that will open at about the same time (this includes a window of two weeks before and one week after the selected date)? The goal here is to avoid competition that will steal a proportion of the core audience.

Media and Advertising

Given the target markets for the film's playability and marketability, which media are most appropriate, given what is available in each territory where the film is to open? It is also important to identify the other films with which a film's trailer should be playing, so that its target audience is reached in the most effective manner.

Several specific tools can be used to achieve these goals.

Research screenings will enable audience response to be tested thoroughly. The audiences at such special screenings, held in advance of a film's release, will be primarily composed of "avids," filmgoers who attend the cinema at least once a fortnight and who are highly influential in distributing word-of-mouth on a film. Those invited to attend such screenings will consist of both the film's target audience and a much wider cross-section of the population.

Positioning analysis will be used to identify those marketing elements that most interest people by evaluating the appeal of each element in relation to all other elements. The goals of positioning analysis are to determine the most opportune date for the film's release, to identify which media will be most effective in reaching a film's target audience, and to test the appeal of selected marketing hooks before a marketing campaign is created.

Such creative materials as print advertising, posters, and trailers will also be tested during market research. This testing is often the most costly portion of the process because many revisions will be made to the materials and each revision will, in turn, be thoroughly tested. The sheer expense of such research puts it beyond the reach of many smaller film distributors.

Research companies will also engage in movie tracking, in which a major film's advertising is tracked for five weeks before the film's release and for several weeks after to evaluate whether its advertising is hitting its intended target. In effect, this measures awareness of a film. Respondents are asked whether the advertising has made them desire to see the film, thus it also measures interest in the picture.

In Europe, such big European companies as PolyGram and Pathé and the distribution subsidiaries of the U.S. majors may use market research to better position a film in a particular market. UIP also uses exit polls in the first two or three markets where a film is released to determine the likely effectiveness of its marketing campaign in other territories.

■ The Publicity and the Promotional Campaign

To counterbalance their competitive disadvantage against the U.S. majors, European independent distributors complement their advertising with publicity and promotion. Publicity and promotion are marketing tools of equal if not greater importance than advertising. Therefore, understanding how they operate is important.

The publicity campaign's goal is to secure editorial coverage for a

> *" Publicity can be a much cheaper method of securing public attention for a film than paid advertising, but the two approaches will usually be used in tandem. "*

specific film in the media that will be seen by the film's target audience. Publicity can be a much cheaper method of securing public attention for a film than paid advertising, but the two approaches will usually be used in tandem because publicity will support the advertising expenditure.

A film's publicist or press attaché will seek to arrange interviews between selected media and the film's director and stars. The publicist will also widely circulate publicity materials to the media and arrange press screenings for the purposes of securing reviews and promoting word-of-mouth recommendations.

A film's publicity campaign will often be handled by a public relations company that specializes in the film industry. However, many European publicists are individuals who work on a freelance basis, and some larger distributors have their own in-house publicists. Some distributors hire different press officers for each film, choosing them according to their taste, their approach to a specific film, and their creativity and relations with the press.

The amount of press coverage a film receives will depend on the film's subject matter (a story that has topical relevance is always a plus), its cast, its director, and, of course, the publicist's contacts in the media, and their ability to place stories. With the fierce competition for film coverage in the print and audiovisual media, publicists have to be creative—especially in the case of specialized films—in finding different angles for different publications and different media.

Promotion is intimately linked to publicity and advertising activities and is often coordinated by the same individuals who are responsible for marketing. Like the publicity campaign, the ultimate goal of the promotional effort is to increase awareness, want-to-see, and word-of-mouth. Promotion covers activities ranging from premieres intended to build word-of-mouth to the licensing and merchandising of characters or objects drawn from a film.

Following is an examination of various strategies for maximizing the effectiveness of publicity and promotional campaigns.

Creating the Strategy

A publicist's first task is to secure coverage for a film in the entertainment and arts sections of the targeted media. This coverage will be determined by the way in which a film has been positioned and by the profile of its target audience. To maximize the chances of securing coverage, a publicist will try to make a film a newsworthy event, which may help secure coverage in the news or political sections of a newspaper in addition to its coverage in the entertainment section. In the case of a specialized film, this can help it cross over to a wider audience.

Journalists and editors are always looking for stories that will sell their publications, so the publicist's task is to convince them that he has something that will interest their readers. In their battle for editorial space, film publicists may face competition not only from other films but also from a wide range of general-interest stories. Therefore, publicists should approach journalists as early as possible.

> *" Journalists and editors are always looking for stories that will sell their publications. "*

The strategy for obtaining media coverage is constructed by the distributor, the publicist, and the promoter. They will consider what type of media coverage is most appropriate for a film, when interviews can best be coordinated with its stars, and when to show a film to the media. The publicity campaign begins, ideally, three to six months before a film's opening.

The publicist is heavily dependent on the quality of the materials provided by the producer, the distributor, or the sales company, with photographs being particularly important. If stills have not been prepared in advance or their quality is poor, the effectiveness of the publicity campaign can be seriously undermined. (This once again highlights the importance of ensuring that unit photographers are attached to films, and that these photographers secure high-quality stills.)

During a film's pre-release period, its publicist will track the available publicity materials, assemble a press kit, organize press screenings,

142

Marketing and
Selling
Your Film
Around the
World

and check the availability of the film's stars and director and prepare their schedule of interviews.

The Press Kit's Ingredients

A publicist should ideally commence work on a film at least three to four months before that film's release. Among a film publicist's very first tasks is the assembly of a press kit for the printed media, including such materials as stills, CD audio and CD-ROM combining the film's original score, scenes from the shooting, a teaser trailer, and other visuals from the film.

Press kits for the printed media usually include cast and credits lists, production notes, stills, and biographies and filmographies of the cast, the director, and the producer. They should also contain details of the film's release. Electronic press kits (EPKs) will contain many of the same items together with selected video clips (for television) and audio clips (for radio).

The publicist will usually use the press kits made by the international sales or the foreign distribution company as a starting point because the varying practices in different countries often require a publicist to adapt materials to meet specific needs. In France, for example, filmographies of cast and crew are preferred to biographies.

Once these press kits have been assembled and adapted to meet each territory's special requirements, they will be distributed to the national and local presses and television and radio journalists. They may also be sent to regional exhibitors for distribution to other local media and to help in their own campaigns.

The Importance of Star Interviews

Interviews with stars and directors are an asset to film promotion. Box-office returns are usually higher for a film that has been promoted in different territories by its stars and its director.

The publicity generated by a mainstream film is usually based around the film's stars and can be used to complement its advertising campaign. For such a picture, the distributor should try to ensure that its major stars undertake press tours, visiting as many territories where the film is to be released as possible for interviews with the local media.

Alternatively, a film's stars can be made available for press junkets in which selected journalists are flown to a particular location for interviews. Such trips are often funded by the distributors themselves, and the resulting coverage is judged to justify the cost of events.

The major studios usually have greater leverage with stars than do independent distributors because stars often have long-term relationships with particular studio executives or on-going production deals with particular studios. The independents simply do not have these alliances, so they must be more inventive in their efforts to secure the promotional support of a film's talent.

For arthouse films, publicity will often focus on the director, if he or she is sufficiently well known, or certain creative aspects of the film. For unknown talent and first-time directors, getting media coverage is difficult, although, in some cases, the media like to discover new talent. "If the media, especially in France, feel that a film made by relative unknowns is interesting, they are prepared to give it space," says French producer and press agent Simona Benzakein.

Press Screenings

Press screenings are primarily aimed at journalists who wish to review a film, although they also serve the useful secondary function of spreading word-of-mouth among the media. Press screenings will often be held at preview theaters, which are small cinemas devoted to such events.

These screenings will need to be organized well in advance of a film's release because both the print and the audiovisual media have deadlines that fall a considerable time before their publication dates. This gap between the deadline and the publication date is known as "lead time." Sufficient lead time must be allowed for each of the various types of publications to file their reviews. For any one film, several press screenings, each aimed at a particular category of publication, may have to be organized. The lead time for various types of publications will tend to vary as follows:

• For monthly magazines, a screening should occur as much as three months ahead of a film's release date if such magazines are to include that film in their issues that hit the newsstands concurrent with the film's release.

• For weekly publications, screenings can occur one month ahead of a film's release.

• For daily publications, screenings can occur as little as two to three days before a film's release.

Radio and television stations will work to their own specific deadlines in advance of the airing of their broadcasts, so special screenings for these media must also be scheduled by the publicist.

Timing is critical. "If you show the film to the media at the wrong moment, they may write about it in a very different way than if you show it to them at a more effective time," says Dutch producer San Fu Maltha.

Some distributors may prefer to keep a film under wraps until the last possible moment to heighten the sense that its release is an event. This approach may also be used to avoid the spread of bad word-of-mouth if a film is likely to be poorly reviewed.

Another effective strategy has the publicist organize private screenings for two to three selected journalists from daily newspapers, who may start generating some early favorable opinions, although their reviews may not appear until nearer the film's release date. These opinion formers, who will be hand-picked by the publicist to try to ensure a positive reaction to the film, may influence both the general public and other journalists.

Even a mainstream picture with a large advertising budget can suffer heavily if critics respond negatively to it. In such a case, an effective advertising and publicity campaign may be the only way to overcome, if only partially, the impact of bad reviews on a film's likely box-office performance.

Preview Screenings

Preview screenings are used to reinforce publicity and advertising activities. Since they are designed to ensure that word-of-mouth peaks with a film's release, they are held at any time from three weeks to just a few days ahead of release. Such screenings are usually free, and often jointly promoted with local radio stations and newspapers, which assist in giving away tickets.

Several different types of preview screenings are common: those for targeted groups of people, those that feature appearances by a film's director and/or stars, and those that are arranged for a film's backers or other private companies that may be involved with the picture.

When setting up preview screenings, a distributor must identify those opinion-makers who will exercise the most powerful influence over a specific target audience, because many preview screenings will be aimed at parts of the population that are felt to be among a film's core audience, and who will help to spread word-of-mouth among their peers. For instance, for a specialized film like *Cyrano de Bergerac*, promotional screenings were aimed at students at colleges and schools, many of whom would be studying the original play, and teachers whose colleagues might well have a strong interest in seeing a film based on such classic material. The tickets for such screenings are distributed directly to selected academic institutions.

As mentioned above, independent distributors who organize preview screenings may also try to reach a targeted audience by giving away tickets in conjunction with the media. Radio stations are often utilized for films that are aimed at youthful audiences because their listeners have the correct age profile. With a radio promotion, tickets to preview screenings might be given to the first listeners to call in and correctly answer some simple questions tied to the film's theme. Such give-aways help radio stations attract listeners. Competitions in newspapers or weekly magazines are often used in the same way.

Screenings that are attended by the film's director or stars can also be very effective for generating interest among particular target audiences and the media.

The practice of preview screening has developed rapidly in Europe in the last few years. However, it has always been used heavily by the subsidiaries of the U.S. majors in Europe, who might hold up to 200 previews across the continent for films that they feel have weak want-to-see because the subject matter is not likely to be of immediate appeal

146

MARKETING AND
SELLING
YOUR FILM
AROUND THE
WORLD

to European audiences (for example, *A League of Their Own,* about baseball, a sport not commonly played in Europe).

The U.S. majors and the larger independent distributors are in a strong position to coordinate previews because they have easy access to screens, the financial resources to create additional prints, and strong negotiating power with the media. For them, spending money on free screenings is part of an overall marketing strategy that is geared toward building audience awareness and word of mouth, with the goal of maximizing admissions during a film's opening days.

Many smaller, independent distributors are increasingly using preview screenings. However, previews are still shunned by some distributors who claim that such screenings invariably reach the same target group–those people who enter competitions in newspapers or on the radio–regardless of what type of film is screened.

Gala Premieres

Gala premieres are prestigious evenings where a film's cast and crew and guests are invited to see it at a prestigious cinema a few days in advance of its release.

The goal of the gala premiere is to secure media coverage of the event and, by extension, increase awareness of the film among cinemagoers. Therefore, the presence of journalists, photographers, and television crews is essential, because they will report about the event in widely circulated magazines and gossip columns. In Spain, the U.K., and certain other European countries, royalty is commonly invited to major premieres, boosting these events' media profiles.

Although such premieres can greatly increase a film's editorial coverage, they tend to be very expensive and will therefore be confined to films with high P&A budgets.

Merchandising Campaigns

A merchandising campaign employs products that reinforce a film's image or identity. Such products can range from simple T-shirts to interactive video games based on a film. For the creation of simple merchandising items, distributors might handle the task themselves. However, with items such as toys, a film's producer will often license the rights to certain motifs and characters from the film to an independent toy manufacturer or merchandise company.

> "A merchandising campaign employs products that reinforce a film's image or identity."

A merchandising campaign serves a two-fold purpose: It raises awareness of a film among its target audience and creates an additional revenue stream for the film's producer, since the licensing of rights can be very lucrative.

Such campaigns will usually be most effective for mainstream pictures, although innovative merchandising may sometimes be effective for more specialized titles. The promotional campaigns for films from the U.S. majors are increasingly associated with the merchandising of products derived from them. At the high-budget end of the market, the American blockbuster *Jurassic Park*, with a $60 million marketing campaign, was launched internationally by distributor UIP with 100 tie-ins–from T-shirts and toys to interactive video games, all of which drew on aspects of the film. Most European distributors are unlikely to handle films that have such a large number of potential tie-ins. However, merchandising campaigns are increasingly popular in Europe: In France, in 1994, such campaigns accounted for some ten percent of most films' promotional budgets. This figure has now risen to thirty percent (and fifty percent for certain films).

When creating a merchandising campaign, staying within the spirit of the film is important. The most common tie-ins are the book on which a film is based and the film's soundtrack, both of which should be released simultaneously with the film's opening and use visual images from the film's poster campaign.

The music soundtrack, an increasingly important tie-in for many theatrical releases, can be a very important means of broadening the awareness of a particular film among its core audience. The benefit of a successful music tie-in is that the film promotes the music and the music promotes the film. The airplay of a particular track or album serves to maintain the public's awareness of the film from which it is taken. Film soundtracks can also be used as promotional items and prizes for competitions and can be featured in point-of-sale displays in record shops that are targeted predominantly at the 15-through-24 age group.

Joint promotions with shops or department stores, in which shop windows are arranged to evoke a scene or a character from a film, can also be exploited. This type of promotion can be used for many different types of films.

The development of interactive media has led to an increase in the potential number of licensing and merchandising opportunities. In the future, many more interactive games will likely be based upon characters derived from films. Even the growth of virtual reality technology has presented filmmakers with new opportunities to license their characters for entertainment-based games. The U.S. majors are already exploring the possibilities in such areas, but independents could also benefit from whatever openings may arise in this area.

Sponsorship

As with tie-ins and promotions, distributors are increasingly turning to sponsorship as a means of offsetting their P&A costs.

In a promotional campaign that involves a record or book tie-in, the distributor will receive the respective merchandise in return for joint promotions. By contrast, sponsorship entails a distributor receiving financial assistance or airplay in return for placing a particular sponsor's logo onto a film's advertising and promotional material. Such material could include posters, trailers, brochures, and such clothing as jackets and caps.

Sponsorship will invariably come from companies that manufacture consumer durables and seek to reach the same audience demographic as a particular film.

Having examined how a distributor creates a strategy for marketing and advertising a film, it is now time to look at the exhibitor's role in a film's marketing.

EXHIBITION IN EUROPE

Section 6

The cinema operator, also known as the exhibitor, is the key link between a film and its audience. His task is to attract the public into *his* cinema to see a movie (while the distributor's task is to persuade the public to attend a particular film at any cinema). The distributor and the exhibitor will work together closely to create a marketing strategy that will achieve their individual and mutual goals. The following section examines the strategies used by exhibitors to ensure that they maximize their revenues.

■ New Cinemas, Rising Admissions

Until the mid-1980s, cinema chains in many countries, notably Germany, Italy, and the U.K., had received little in the way of investment and, as a consequence, fell into a state of disrepair, with poor seating and low-quality screens. This problem primarily plagued the cinemas owned by large chains, although it also often plagued many independent or arthouse cinemas. Management standards were often poor both at a national level and within individual cinemas. Few cinemas had the ability to take credit-card bookings from customers, and most cinemas had a limited range of concessions and low standards of cleanliness. The only major territory that was an exception to this rule was France, where the vitality of their domestic cinema industry and the public's keen interest in films meant that their major chains, such as Gaumont, UGC, and Pathé, maintained a program of continuous investment in cinema maintenance.

The Introduction of the Multiplex

While cinema-attendance levels in many European countries plummeted, few exhibitors seemed to make the causal connection between this and the poor physical state of many cinemas, preferring to blame declining attendance on the growth of such ancillary media as television and video. Among those who suffered most heavily from this decline in admissions were the Hollywood-based major distributors. As a result, the U.S. majors took the lead in the move to rejuvenate the European exhibition industry.

In the U.K., for example, the number of cinema screens have risen from 1,530 in 1980 to 2,383 in 1997 (see Chart 3), a sixty-four percent increase.[1] This growth has been driven principally by the construction of new multiplex sites, although some twenty percent of the $1.65 billion spent on cinema building and improvements since 1985 has been invested in the refurbishment of traditional sites. However, with an estimated 37.6 screens per million people, the U.K. still lags considerably behind such countries as the U.S. (111.6 screens per million), France (77 screens per million), and Germany (48.9 screens per million).[2]

When discussing the growth of cinema attendance in the U.K., the greater availability of attractive, well-marketed films, which have also been a key factor in the rejuvenation of the cinema industry, should be stressed. While the reversal of the U.K.'s admissions decline is commonly attributed solely to the impact of multiplexes, it is worth noting that the most dramatic rise in admissions occurred when they rose from 54 million in 1984 to 72 million in 1985. Since The Point, Britain's first multiplex (built by American Multi-Cinema), did not open until November 1985, there is little doubt that the popularity of Hollywood blockbusters, notably *Ghostbusters*, played a significant part in driving this early rise in admissions.

The arrival of a limited number of new multiplexes over the next five years will further boost numbers, although there are doubts in some countries as to whether many would-be operators of megaplexes will be able to secure the necessary planning approval. Already, France has introduced limits on the size of new multiplexes. In the traditional cinema sector, the increase caused by the construction of new venues will most likely be somewhat offset by the closure of existing venues.

---

[1]Dodona Research, *Cinemagoing 5*, (Leicester, Dodona Research, 1996), p. 1.
[2]Figures for overseas countries are 1995 figures taken from *Screen Digest* (August, 1997).

The Multiplexes' Impact on Film Distribution

The increase in the number of available screens in Europe, as a result of the impact of multiplexes, has not, so far, lead to a commensurate increase in the number of release slots available for individual films. Therefore, while distributors can secure initial bookings for a film, holding over a film that is performing relatively well for more than a few weeks sometimes proves difficult because of the sheer volume of product jostling for space in the marketplace. Every week, four to eight new movies come into the marketplace and compete for screen space. And as the volume of new titles coming into the market increases, distributors will be

> *"Increasing the volume of screens in the market does not necessarily lead to an increase in the variety of titles available to cinemagoers."*

tempted to open films as widely as possible as early as possible. In short, increasing the volume of screens does not necessarily lead to an increase in the variety of titles available to cinemagoers or new opportunities for distributors.

A number of operators have plans to segment their larger venues, setting aside particular screens for more specialized movies, so that a greater variety of product can be shown within a given venue. In some cases, operators will brand these screens with a distinct identity and even give them their own separate entrances and foyers. This is likely to benefit independent films–including those from the U.S.–that tend to be oriented toward a niche or arthouse audience. Although, this is only likely to happen in those venues that have twenty or more screens.

Current indicators suggest that mainstream product will go out with an increasing number of prints in the future. Even though, on the bigger films, multiplexes can use one print for two or more screens, some venues may wish to use separate prints for the biggest releases, so that they can offer staggered start times for those titles. In any case,

154

MARKETING AND
SELLING
YOUR FILM
AROUND THE
WORLD

as the number of prints grows, distributors will be able to benefit from volume discounts so that the incremental costs of striking extra prints will be relatively low.

The Nature of the Multiplex

The multiplex typically comprises eight to ten screens. The first wave of European multiplexes, which were built during the late 1980s, were generally constructed on the outskirts of towns and cities.

The pioneers in multiplex building in Europe were Belgium's Bert family. With three generations of cinema exhibitors before him and the desire to offer audiences the same comfort as they might find in their own homes, but with better sound (digital) and better visibility (70mm prints), Albert Bert began the transformation of a one-screen cinema into a triplex in 1972. With another family (Claeys), he also built what was to become the biggest multiscreen complex in Europe, the Kinepolis.

American Multi-Cinema (AMC) was the first to introduce multiplexes in the U.K. with the development of its site in Milton Keynes, north of London, in 1985. Many European groups, such as Virgin in the U.K., Flebbe Filmtheater in Germany, and UGC, Gaumont, and Pathé in France are involved in multiplex building and cinema refurbishment as a means of staying competitive.

While multiplex cinemas have been the main engine of growth in the European exhibition sector, European arthouse cinemas, the majority of which are independently owned, have also played a role in driving up overall cinema attendance. Traditionally, most arthouse cinemas have relied heavily on arthouse pictures. But in the face of the increasing share of the European box office that is being snared by large U.S. films, many independents have had to adopt a more varied programming diet to remain viable. While predominantly European-originated art films still tend to form the backbone of programming for these cinemas, many have started to show selected "quality" films from Hollywood, such as *The English Patient.*

In the last ten years, many arthouse operators in Europe have spent money on refurbishing their cinemas in the face of competition from the new multiplex operators and the established chains that have been revamping their theaters. To compete with the multiplexes, arthouse cinemas must not only show a different type of film but must also provide a different type of experience. For instance, realizing that many spectators are irked by cinema commercials, the screens owned by the independent distributor Alta Films in Spain do not carry advertising, a policy that is common to many independents throughout Europe.

Some arthouse cinemas will offer such additional facilities as cafés or restaurants or bookshops. Cafés are an increasingly common feature of independent cinemas throughout Europe, and they may often be open to people who are not going to see a film. In many cases, these cafés will offer a full meal, often with an emphasis on health food, which is likely to appeal to their prospective audience. As a consequence, there is less reliance on such concessions as popcorn and hot dogs.

The decor of these cinemas may also be geared toward a more upmarket audience. The restaurant space at some arthouse cinemas is decorated with film memorabilia, creating surroundings that are likely to appeal to an educated audience with an appreciation of cinema history. Some cinemas also stock film books to enhance the sense of cinematic tradition and provide a useful source of additional revenue for the venue.

For both multiplexes and arthouse cinemas, box-office receipts alone are sometimes insufficient to provide the exhibitor a profit. Therefore, screen advertising, shown prior to a film's start, and sales of such concessions as confectionery and soft drinks, offer a lucrative source of additional revenue. As a rule of thumb, concessions sales in traditional cinemas will be equal to fifteen percent of the box-office gross. For multiplex cinemas, the figure may be as high as twenty-two to twenty-three percent. This figure has risen from ten

> *" For both multiplex and arthouse cinemas, box-office receipts alone are sometimes insufficient to give the exhibitor a profit. "*

percent as such labor-intensive practices as auditorium sales have been replaced by kiosk sales.

Gross margins on concessions may be as high as sixty-five to seventy percent, and as high as eighty percent on such top-selling items as Coke and popcorn. A concessions sales figure of $1.50 per admission might be achieved by a multiplex chain; a more traditional chain might generate $1.20 per admission. Both concessions and advertising are far more important components of an exhibitor's income than they were prior to the advent of multiplexes. Thus, maximizing revenues from concession sales is a priority for most exhibitors.

Screen advertising has also proved to be a lucrative source of additional income for exhibitors. The sale of screen advertising is usually handled either by the chain itself or by an independent sales house. Although this advertising provides an income boost for cinema chains, some producers and distributors are concerned that excessive amounts of advertising may deter audiences. Several chains in Europe have introduced limitations on the amount of advertising they carry, although the economic importance of screen advertising makes many exhibitors reluctant to pursue such a policy.

■ Marketing Strategies

If distributors are to maximize a film's chances of performing well at the cinema, they must maintain good relationships with the film bookers who work for the cinema chains. Some chains will have one national booker, supplemented by a number of regional bookers who are responsible for a particular local area. The regional bookers are in constant contact with local cinema managers who relay information about audience reaction to certain types of films and particular stars. In the case of smaller chains and independent cinemas, the managing director or owner of the company will often personally take responsibility for booking films.

Although bookers will generally be willing to book big-name films without seeing them, few bookers will be prepared to take this risk on smaller, more specialized pictures. Most mainstream pictures will be booked three to six months in advance of their release, although major U.S. blockbusters will be booked up to a year in advance.

Booking a film less than three months ahead of its release usually leaves insufficient time to prepare fully its marketing campaign. Nevertheless, it is common practice, particularly in the case of smaller films. In some smaller countries, even large cinema chains tend to book most of their films just two months in advance of release.

Because delivery times of films are often subject to change, bookers must constantly revise their opening dates. However, arthouse exhibitors tend to be more rigid in their booking policies. They will usually book a film for a minimum period of four to six weeks, and as long as the take exceeds the "house nut" (the overhead costs of running the cinema, including rent, heat, electricity, staff, etc.), it will not be taken off the screen to make way for another picture.

After viewing a film, an exhibitor will meet with the film's distributor to discuss a release pattern. In some cases, the distributor may have to exert pressure on the exhibitor, because the latter may be reluctant to take a certain number of prints or to offer particular screens. This is particularly the case with specialized pictures, because exhibitors are often unwilling to take risks on such films. Exhibitors will offer such films unattractive opening dates or short-notice playdates that allowing too little time for the development of an effective marketing campaign.

The distributor-exhibitor relationship is a two-way street, and exhibitors may also face problems when negotiating with distributors. The practice of block booking, under which larger distributors will only guarantee cinema chains their hit titles if those exhibitors also agree to book some weaker or less-successful pictures, is privately acknowledged as a constant problem for exhibitors in some territories (although few are willing to denounce the practice publicly). However, exhibitors can do little to resist block booking because the larger distributors control the supply of hit films that are the lifeblood of most cinema chains.

Ideally, distributors and exhibitors would work together and coordinate their marketing campaigns to benefit a given film, but, as is

"The respective goals of distributors and exhibitors often give rise to conflict."

somewhat obvious, the respective goals of distributors and exhibitors often give rise to conflict: Exhibitors usually want their cinema to make money with popular movies, regardless of which movies these may be. So, if a film doesn't do well on its opening weekend, they will take it off the screen and show another film instead. Distributors, on the other hand, want a film to stay in release for as long as possible. Arthouse films, in particular, need a long run to establish themselves through word-of-mouth, but exhibitors are not always willing to give such films the opportunity to reach their full potential.

A distributor who owns cinemas has the singular advantage of being able to control a film's hold-over, keeping it on screen longer than an exhibitor might do in normal circumstances. Another advantage for distributors who are also exhibitors is, in most instances, their ability to book their own films for preferred dates. Since a shortage of screens exists in many European markets, many distributors, especially the smaller companies, often have to wait a considerable amount of time before they can open their films.

Distributors should try to ensure that their marketing efforts are supplemented by similar efforts on the part of the exhibitors, which will allow a film the best possible chance of maximizing its target audience.

A film's distributor is responsible for handling its trailer, its poster, and any television advertising campaigns. Few exhibitors will have direct input into the construction of these campaigns, although in some countries they will be asked to bear some of the cost of the prints and advertising. In Switzerland, for instance, exhibitors are expected to fund fifty percent of the costs of local advertising, which is equivalent to ten to fifteen percent of the entire P&A budget. The distributor will bear the costs of all other advertising.

A marketing effort should not end with the distributor. The exhibitor can also play a key role in helping to promote a film to the public. The most common form of marketing that an exhibitor will undertake is the purchasing of space in local newspapers to advertise the films they are screening. These advertisements will often appear on the day of the film's change over (often a Friday) because many chains will do anywhere from thirty to sixty percent

> *"The marketing effort should not end with the distributor. The exhibitor can also play a key role in helping to promote the film to the public."*

of their business during the weekend. Only in very rare instances will an exhibitor use television advertising because the cost of this advertising is simply prohibitive.

Involving local exhibitors in a film's promotion can pay handsome dividends. Many cinema chains try to ensure that the local managers of each cinema in the group are in close contact with the local media during the two months leading up to a film's release. These managers will prepare marketing plans for their cinemas, based on a specific marketing hook.

If any aspect of a picture has a local hook—for example, a film's content may relate in some way to the local area—this can be used

> *"Involving local exhibitors in a film's promotion can pay handsome dividends."*

to maximize its marketing potential. The marketing plan may involve identifying certain key sites for advertising the film or creating a ticket give-away contest in partnership with a local paper or retail store, which will ensure editorial coverage of the film in the local paper. The aim of this is to convey information about the date and time when the film will screen, give the public a flavor of the picture, maximize awareness of the picture, and stimulate want-to-see. A number of other, more general strategies may also be used by exhibitors to promote both specific films and the idea of cinemagoing in general. Wherever possible, distributors should encourage exhibitors to explore the possibility of such promotions since they will benefit both parties.

When dealing with larger productions, some chains may invite all their cinema managers to a talk given by the film's star or director. Such events will also provide an opportunity for the managers to be

160

Marketing and
Selling
Your Film
Around the
World

photographed with the star or the director, providing useful publicity material for the local media.

One form of marketing frequently undertaken by cinema chains is the production of a magazine or newsletter that provides information about their forthcoming releases. Such publications are usually glossy, four-color productions financed by advertising and distributed to patrons in the cinema foyer. In some instances, chains may even charge patrons a fee for such publications.

To boost cinema admissions, some exhibitors are starting to explore the promotion of the idea of cinemagoing. Campaigns for this can include the use of slogans (on posters and such other merchandise as sweatshirts) encouraging people to go to the cinema.

Such promotional initiatives as the Fête du Cinéma in France and the Festa del Cinema in Italy, which were discussed earlier in this book, are also proving successful in both raising attendance during specific periods of the year and boosting the profile of cinemagoing as a leisure activity, especially for individuals who may fall outside the core cinemagoers' demographics. On a somewhat smaller scale, some exhibitors organize mini-festivals that are designed to promote certain types of films.

In an attempt to attract older audiences, the Svenskfilmindustri chain in Sweden sells cinema tickets to large companies that can give them away to their employees. UCI in the U.K. has made strenuous attempts to attract the thirty-five-plus age group into cinemas by offering such services as advanced seat booking and credit-card payment and by ensuring that each of their locations offers a broad range of programming. As a result of such efforts, the demographic of the average British cinemagoer has broadened beyond the fifteen to twenty-five age bracket. This broadening has been accompanied by an increased demand for independent films, because more mature audiences predominantly favor more sophisticated films of the type handled by independents.

Some European exhibitors, especially arthouse chains, use direct marketing to reach potential customers, regularly mailing their customers programs that detail their forthcoming films. Direct marketing allows cinemas to market to particular types of audiences for particular types of films, providing a highly effective means of targeting certain groups.

Different forms of ticket pricing can also be used by the exhibitor to encourage the public into the cinema. The most popular ticket-pricing innovation in recent years has been the introduction of a particular day each week when ticket prices are reduced across the board. Such discounts are employed by both the large chains and the independent cinemas. The day when such discounts are offered varies widely across Europe.

Once an audience is inside the cinema, the screening of trailers can be a very effective way of persuading them to return to see forthcoming films. Here the distributor must work as closely as possible with the exhibitor to ensure that a trailer's impact of is maximized, since many cinemas are reluctant to play trailers, which, unlike screen advertising, do not offer an immediate source of income. As a result, as much as seventy-five percent of the screen time that precedes a film's screening will be given over to advertising and only twenty-five percent to trailers, which only allows enough time for two or three trailers to be shown.

However, the under-utilization of trailers is not purely the fault of the exhibitor. The lengths of many contemporary films create problems. Ten years ago, the average film's length was ninety minutes; now it is closer to 120 minutes. As films get longer, showing a varied number of trailers becomes more difficult because the feature presentation must to be screened a certain number of times each day.

Exhibitors want to strike the right balance between attracting an audience to future presentations and maintaining its appetite for the film that it has paid to see. As a result, some chains deliberately restrict the length of time allotted for trailers. Few European exhibitors play more than ten minutes of trailers before a film. Because of the exhibitors' reluctance to spend too much time showing trailers, trailer lengths becomes critical. The shorter they are, the more likely the exhibitor is to screen them. In many cases, shorter trailers are also more likely to have an impact on cinemagoers. For both these reasons, a sharp, punchy thirty-second trailer that singles out a few dramatic moments in a film could be much more effective than a three-minute version that attempts to encapsulate its entire story.

In some European territories, attempts are underway to use trailers in more innovative ways. For example, some exhibitors have introduced free weekly trailer shows to give their audiences a foretaste of coming attractions. Regardless of how one goes about presenting trailers, the underlying philosophy is simple: Ensure that trailers are shown to the maximum number of people possible, because trailers will help instill a regular cinemagoing habit in the public.

A distributor's timely delivery of a trailer to an exhibitor is crucial to securing its maximum impact on audiences. Ideally, a film's trailer should start showing two months before the film's release, yet some exhibitors complain that the distributor often delivers the trailer just four weeks prior to the film's release, which often means that the film's potential audience will only see its trailer once or twice, dulling the trailer's impact on the cinemagoer. Teaser trailers should be delivered two to three months in advance of the film's release.

> *" A distributor's timely delivery of a trailer to an exhibitor is crucial to securing its maximum impact on audiences. "*

■ Reporting

Once a film has opened, each cinema chain must provide that film's distributor with a regular and detailed report of the money earned by that film at their individual cinemas. This process, which is called "reporting," should be very closely monitored by the distributor. Accuracy is vital because this reporting is the basis for the allocation of revenues among the exhibitor, the distributor, the producer, and any other parties (such as the star or the director) who may have an equity interest in the film.

During a film's opening week, most cinemas will report their gross box office to the distributor on a daily basis. These figures will be sent by fax or telephoned in.

During a film's opening days, particularly during its opening weekend, reporting is critical, because this is the first opportunity for both the distributor and the cinema chain to assess the likely run of a given film in a given territory. A film's reviews, which will usually be published a few days before its release, may offer a clue to a picture's potential appeal to the public, but not until the exhibitor reveals a film's opening figures can an informed forecast of its likely performance be made. Since films invariably perform most strongly in their opening week and admissions usually decrease gradually from the second

> *" Not until the exhibitor reveals a film's opening figures can an informed forecast of its likely performance be made. "*

week onward, it is possible to extrapolate considerable information from these opening figures.

In some countries, such as Belgium, Germany, and Sweden, one group, acting on behalf of the distributors, is responsible for collecting all the box-office information and disseminating it. The advantage of using such independent groups to collect box-office information is that it becomes much harder for the various parties involved to distort figures consistently, since the collection group will have a detailed knowledge of the grosses achieved by individual cinemas.

Net Rentals

The percentage of the box-office gross that is returned to the distributor is known as the "net rental" share. Before calculating the distributor's share of the box-office gross, the cinema operator first deducts his expenses from the total gross.

Clearly, the costs of running cinemas vary widely, depending on location, number of screens, labor costs, and several other factors. Therefore, the net rental share varies widely across Europe. The actual method for calculating rentals and their actual level varies country by country for a variety of historical reasons.

In the 1996 *European Cinema Yearbook*, Media Salles compiled figures to illustrate the average levels of rentals in selected territories.[3] These figures differ from some of the industry estimates discussed above, indicating the difficulty of securing authoritative information on the exact level of rentals.

TABLE 3.1

Average Level of Film Rentals as Percentage of Box Office Gross in Selected European Territories 1989-1995

SOURCE: Media Salles (some figures approximate according to original source).

	1989	1990	1991	1992	1993	1994	1995
AUSTRIA	44%	40%	36%	38%	38%	n/a	35%
DENMARK	43%	42%	41%	42%	43%	43%	42%
FRANCE	47.4%	47.6%	47.2%	47%	46.9%	48.4%	48.8%
GERMANY	40.3%	43.4%	41.2%	42.4%	43.7%	43.8%	45.2%
IRELAND	44%	42%	n/a	38%	n/a	n/a	38%
ITALY	42%	42%	42%	42%	42%	40%	38.6%
THE NETHERLANDS	38.6%	37.1%	37%	39%	40.4%	40.1%	39.5%
NORWAY	38%	37%	37%	41%	37%	37%	36%
SPAIN	n/a	n/a	n/a	n/a	n/a	n/a	52%
SWEDEN	40%	40%	40%	n/a	40-45%	40-45%	40-45%

These figures suggest that the average level of rentals across Europe is somewhere between forty-two and forty-five percent.

---

[3] *European Cinema Yearbook*, (Milan, Cinema D'Europa/Media Salles, 1997)

Rental levels are also subject to change. For example, in Germany net rentals have increased over the last ten years from around forty to forty-two percent of the box office in the first four weeks of a film's release to forty-five to fifty percent. In part, this reflects the fact that distributors have been bearing an increased share of the marketing cost of films relative to exhibitors. But by the end of a film's run, its distributor may be taking as little as thirty percent of the total gross.